METHODS OF DISCOVERY

Contemporary Societies Series

Jeffrey C. Alexander, Series Editor

Forthcoming

METHODS OF DISCOVERY

Heuristics for the Social Sciences

Andrew Abbott
UNIVERSITY OF CHICAGO

CONTEMPORARY SOCIETIES
Jeffrey C. Alexander
SERIES EDITOR

 W. W. NORTON & COMPANY ⦵ NEW YORK LONDON

W. W. Norton & Company has been independent since its founding in 1923, when William Warder Norton and Mary D. Herter Norton first published lectures delivered at the People's Institute, the adult education division of New York City's Cooper Union. The Nortons soon expanded their program beyond the Institute, publishing books by celebrated academics from America and abroad. By mid-century, the two major pillars of Norton's publishing program—trade books and college texts—were firmly established. In the 1950s, the Norton family transferred control of the company to its employees, and today—with a staff of four hundred and a comparable number of trade, college, and professional titles published each year—W. W. Norton & Company stands as the largest and oldest publishing house owned wholly by its employees.

Manufacturing by Quebecor World, Fairfield.
Book design by Beth Tondreau.
Production manager: Benjamin Reynolds.

Library of Congress Cataloging-in-Publication Data
Abbott, Andrew Delano.
    Methods of discovery : heuristics for the social sciences / Andrew Abbott.
        p.   cm.— (Contemporary societies)
    Includes bibliographical references and index.

ISBN 0-393-97814-1 (pbk.)

    1. Social sciences—Philosophy.   2. Social sciences—Methodology.   3. Heuristic.
I. Title.   II. Series.

H61.15.A23 2003
300'.1—dc22

                                                                2003061567

W. W. Norton & Company, Inc., 500 Fifth Avenue, New York, N.Y. 10110
www.wwnorton.com

W. W. Norton & Company Ltd., Castle House,
75/76 Wells Street, London W1T 3QT

5   6   7   8   9   0

Cum omnis ratio diligens disserendi duas habeat partis, unam inveniendi alteram iudicandi.

Every systematic treatment of argumentation has two branches, one concerned with invention of arguments and the other with judgment of their validity.

Cicero, Topica 1:6

CONTENTS

ACKNOWLEDGMENTS

THIS LITTLE TEXT has its roots in my book *Chaos of Disciplines*. While writing *Chaos*, I came to realize that my theory of how social science developed also implied a view of how social science should be done. When Jeff Alexander offered me the opportunity to put that vision into writing, I seized it. But the heady notion of fractal heuristics that came from *Chaos of Disciplines* quickly became part of a broader attempt to write something my students needed desperately: an introduction to the workings of imagination in social science. Undergraduate and graduate education in social science is so focused on "making it count" (Lieberson 1985) that we gradually kill the excitement our students bring to their work. I have, I hope, written a book that will show how to protect that excitement, in no small part by showing how practicing social scientists have themselves protected it throughout the last century.

This book was written in the intervals of teaching and rests almost completely on my experience as a teacher supervising papers, theses, and dissertations. First and foremost, then, I thank my classroom and dissertation students at the University of Chicago. They have taught me much: both directly, by what they've told me, and indirectly, by the struggles for which my help was so often unavailing. More particularly, I thank my Sociological Inquiry and Thesis Proposal classes for having helped me clarify these ideas. I hope that this book will capture some hint of the excitement of our conversations. I also thank university audiences at San Diego, Harvard, Oxford, and Oslo, as well as a conference group at the Social Science History Association, all of whom heard and commented on Chapter One.

Much of the book was designed, and large parts of it drafted, during a stay at Nuffield College, Oxford, during Hilary Term 2001. I thank the Warden and Fellows of Nuffield for their support. One chapter (Chapter Six—typically, the first to be imagined was the last to be completed) was written during a short visit, in 2002, to the Department of Sociology at Harvard, whose kind hospitality I acknowledge. Erin York was the research assistant who chased down various sources and resources in time taken from the writing of her own splendid master's paper. Above all, I acknowledge the example of George Pólya, whose book *How to Solve It* first taught me the importance of heuristic. Such success as this book may enjoy derives from his happy inspiration. Its failures—no doubt considerable—are mine.

Chicago, November 2003

To the Reader

IT IS A SURPRISING FACT that many good students, when they sit down to write course papers or bachelor's theses or even doctoral dissertations, fear that they have nothing to say. They understand methods. They know about sources and data. But their own contribution seems to them obvious or trivial.

It is little wonder students feel this way. Faculty stuff literatures and methods into their heads until there is little room for anything else. Of course students think everything has already been said; they just read it last week. And of course they make theoretical arguments by blending ideas from here and there like squirrels furnishing a nest with trash; they haven't learned to create theoretical arguments on their own. Small wonder they feel at a loss.

What then does it take to have something to say? It takes two things. The first is a puzzle, something about the social world that is odd, unusual, unexpected, or novel. The second is a clever idea that responds to or interprets or solves that puzzle. Everything else—the methods, the literature, the description of data—is really just window dressing. The heart of good work is a puzzle and an idea.

Although I shall talk about puzzles in the last chapter, this is chiefly a book about finding ideas. And while I talk about social science methods and about research using those methods,

Methods of Discovery is not really about methods. Instead, it is about the *creativity* that animates methods.

Creativity cannot be taught. As John Dewey put it, "[N]o thought, no idea, can possibly be conveyed as an idea from one person to another" (1966:159). We can teach others the backgrounds, the conditions, and the origins of an idea. But if we tell them the idea itself, they don't really have it. To really have it, they must make it inside themselves. Jane Austen put it a little more bluntly in *Pride and Prejudice*: "We all love to instruct, though we can teach only what is not worth knowing."

Nonetheless, by teaching some basic tricks for producing ideas, I hope to give the reader tools for social scientific discovery. And I will show how these tools for invention and discovery relate to the methods that are—with good reason—thought to be our chief ways of producing competent work.

I have assumed undergraduate students as my basic audience. But much of what I have to say can be useful to graduate students or even the occasional colleague. Writing this book has often reminded me of important things I had myself forgotten (and will forget again, no doubt). We are all on the same journey, all trying to say interesting things, all falling into bad habits, all struggling to imagine the social world anew.

NOTE: I have tried to keep scholarly machinery to a minimum in the text. In general, when the text refers to an author and a title, I have not added further citation if it is not necessary to identify a reference uniquely. All articles and books mentioned in the text appear in the References at the end of the book. I have likewise minimized endnotes as much as possible.

METHODS OF DISCOVERY

Chapter One
EXPLANATION

SCIENCE IS A CONVERSATION between rigor and imagination. What one proposes, the other evaluates. Every evaluation leads to new proposals, and so it goes, on and on.

Many people think of social science less as a conversation than as a monologue. For them, it is a long speech that ends with a formal question, to which reality meekly answers yes or no like the plastic heroine of a Victorian novel. Yet no good researcher believes in such monologues. Researchers know all about the continual interchange between intuition and method, just as they know about the endless teasing of reality as it evades them. Social science in practice is less old-style romance than modern soap opera.

The monologue version of social science is of course easier to describe. There are many excellent books about its machinery:

how to propose a question, how to design a study, how to acquire and analyze data, how to draw inferences. Indeed, many books are organized around particular ways of doing these things, the various "methods," as we call them: ethnography, surveys, secondary data analysis, historical and comparative methods, and so on. All that is fine and good.

But such books forget the other voice, the imaginative voice of whimsy, surprise, and novelty. This discovery side of social science is more systematic than we think. Social scientists use gambits of imagination, mental moves they employ to hasten discovery. Like gambits in chess, these mental moves are formulas for the opening, developing, and realizing of possibilities. Some are general gambits implicit in the nature of argument and description, while others arise in conceptual issues that pervade the disciplines. All of these gambits work within *any* kind of method. They make up the heuristic of social science, the means by which social science discovers new ideas.

We need heuristic because, as I said, social reality often resists the charms of methodology. As social scientists, we aim to say something interesting—perhaps even true—about social life. Yet social reality often makes a stingy reply to even the best of our methodological monologues, returning tiny correlations even though challenged by the best of questionnaires, returning simpleminded truisms even though watched by months of earnest ethnography, returning boring stories even though questioned by years of painstaking archival research. Social reality wants a subtler wooing; it wants rigor *and* imagination.[1]

So this is a book about heuristic, a book of aids to the social scientific imagination. Because I am a sociologist, many of the examples I use in the book come from sociology. But because the social sciences are all mixed up together, not all of the examples will be sociological. The social sciences share subject matters, theories, and a surprising amount of methodology. They are not organized into a clearly defined system but take their orientations from various historical accidents. Loosely speaking, economics is organized by a theoretical concept (the idea of choice under constraint), political science by an aspect of social organization (power), anthropology by a method (ethnography), history by an aspect of temporality (the past), and sociology by a list of subject matters (inequality, the city, the family, and so on). Thus, there is no single criterion for the distinctions among disciplines. As a result, when one or another discipline becomes too much of a bore, the others make fun of it and steal its best ideas to put them to better use elsewhere. All of this flux means that a heuristics book can range widely, as this one will.

THE FIRST TWO CHAPTERS introduce the aims, means, and assumptions of social science research. I begin with explanation because explanation is the purpose of social science. I then introduce some types of methods—some of the various ways in which social scientists have tried to be rigorous. I treat these methods as concrete realizations of "explanatory programs," programs that carry out the different concepts of explanation introduced earlier in the chapter.

Chapter Two turns to a more customary approach. I characterize methods in terms of a set of conceptual issues—nine of them, in fact. I first introduce these conceptual issues, then give the customary account of methods (I skipped it in Chapter One), which says that methods are best defined in terms of these nine issues. Then I leave the beaten path. I discuss the critiques that each method poses to the others and show that these critiques lead us into an endless cycling through the methods (both in theory and in practice). Moreover, the conceptual issues themselves turn out not to be fixed things; they have an unstable, fractal character. Not only do they differentiate one method from another, they also differentiate internal strands *within* each method—and internal strands within the internal strands. And so on.

Chapters One and Two are the heavy lifting before the fun part begins. While the main aim of the book is to stimulate imagination, it needs to present a clear sense of rigor as well. Otherwise, we won't be able to tell the difference between imagination and foolishness. Recognizing that difference means getting a secure sense of what explanation is, of why we seek explanations, and of what different kinds of explanations and programs of explanation exist in social science. It also means having a solid grasp of more traditional ways of thinking about rigor, which are presented in Chapter Two, with its litany of the classic methodological debates in social science and its endless isms. (Ultimately, I will turn these isms from dead methodological debates into live heuristics.)

Having set forth the basics of rigor in Chapters One and Two, I then turn to imagination. Chapter Three discusses the general concept of heuristic and sets forth the two simplest heuristic strategies: the additive heuristic of normal science and the use of commonplace lists to generate new ideas. Chapter Four considers in detail the general heuristic gambits that search for importable novelty elsewhere and produce it by transforming our existing arguments. Chapter Five looks at the heuristics of time and space, the heuristics that change ways of describing or envisioning social reality so as to produce new ideas. Chapter Six examines the gambits that arise out of the basic debates and methodological concerns of Chapter Two—making a positivist move within an interpretive tradition, for example. Finally, Chapter Seven discusses the problem of evaluating the ideas produced by heuristics. It asks how we know a good idea when we see one.

I have drawn examples from as far back as the 1920s and as recently as 1999. Old work is not necessarily bad work. Newton himself is a good example. Newton became the greatest name in modern science by *giving up on* the medieval question of the nature and origins of motion. He solved the problem of motion by simply assuming that (a) motion exists and (b) it tends to persist. By means of these assumptions (really a matter of declaring victory, as we would now put it), he was able to develop and systematize a general account of the regularities of motion in the physical world. That is, by giving up on the *why* question, he almost completely answered the *what* question. So following his example, we learn that switching questions is a powerful heuristic move.

The very same move has occurred in social science. One of the great difficulties in the work of Talcott Parsons, the dominant American sociologist of the mid–twentieth century, was in explaining social change. Parsons held that social behavior was governed by norms, which were themselves governed by values, which were themselves governed by yet more general values. In such a system, change could be conceived only as local breakdown, a problem event that had somehow escaped

the supervising norms. Later writers handled the same problem—explaining change—by simply assuming that social
change was not unusual at all; rather, it was the normal state
of affairs. With this assumption, the various historical sociologists who challenged Parsons were able to develop much more
effective accounts of social movements, of revolutions, and,
indeed, of the rise of modernity in general. This was exactly
the Newtonian move: historical sociologists gave up on explaining change and simply assumed it was happening all the
time. Then all they had to do was figure out what is regular
about the way it happens. (They should have gone on to explain stability, of course, but they pretty much forgot about
that!)

Thus, old work provides useful examples of heuristics just
as new work does. This means that as I introduce the reader
to the basic tool kit of heuristics in social science, I can simultaneously introduce some of the great heritage that that tool
kit has produced. Let's begin, then, at the beginning—with
explanation.

I. EXPLANATION

Social science aims to explain social life. There are three things
that make a social scientist say that a particular argument is an
explanation. First, we say something is an explanation when it
allows us to intervene in whatever it is we are explaining. For
example, we have explained the economy when we can manage
it. We have explained poverty when we know how to eradicate
it.

Second, we say an account explains something when we stop
looking for further accounts of that something. An explanation

is an account that suffices. It frees us to go on to the next problem by bringing our current problem into a commonsense world where it becomes immediately comprehensible. So sociobiologists say they have explained altruistic behavior when they show it to be merely an accidental result of selfish behavior. They go no further because they think selfish behavior is self-evident; it needs no explanation.

Third, we often say we have an explanation of something when we have made a certain kind of argument about it: an argument that is simple, exclusive, perhaps elegant or even counterintuitive. Thus, we may think Freudian psychology is better than folk psychology because it is better worked out, more complex, and more surprising. In this third sense, an account is an explanation because it takes a certain pleasing form, because it somehow marries simplicity and complexity.

The first of these views—the *pragmatic* view that an explanation is an account that enables us to intervene—is the most familiar. Consider the explanation of germ-based disease. We think discovering a germ is explaining a disease because by discovering the germ, we have discovered something that enables us to stop the disease. Note that this pragmatic approach to explanation works best for phenomena that have somewhere a narrow neck of necessary causality: something absolutely necessary to the phenomenon yet clearly defined and subject to outside action. It is this narrow neck—the necessity of a particular organism—that makes the germ-based diseases easier to fight than diseases "caused" by the interaction of millions of small random events—cancer, heart disease, and arthritis. The move to the microcellular level in studying these diseases aims precisely to find a *new* realm where there *may be* a narrow neck—

the necessary presence of a certain gene or enzyme, for example. In social science, however, relatively few phenomena seem to have this narrow-neck pattern. So, as we shall see, the pragmatic approach to explanation in social science has taken a different path.

In the second view of explanation, where an explanation is an account that enables us to stop looking for further accounts, things are different. This kind of explanation works by transposing the thing we want to explain from a world that is less comprehensible to one that is more comprehensible. The attempt to explain all human activities without any reference to group phenomena is a good example. The utilitarian philosophers tried to show that systematic pursuit of self-interest by everyone (an individual phenomenon repeated many times) would, when aggregated, result in the social world that was best for all. Social reality was just an additive total of individual realities. *Apparent* social phenomena, like the (to them unbelievable) phenomenon of people getting along without obvious coordination, *must* be explained as the result of some ensemble of individual behaviors.

This second view of explanation—in which we think explanation is a move from one conceptual world to another—is not a pragmatic but rather a *semantic* view. It defines explanation as *translating* a phenomenon from one sphere of analysis to another until a final realm is reached with which we are intuitively satisfied. So the utilitarians "explain" prosocial behavior as an outcome of individual selfishness because they feel the latter realm—that of individual selfish activity—is more real, more intuitive, than any other. It doesn't need to be explained any further. It is a "final realm" for explanation.

Of course, different schools of thought have different final realms for explanation. Utilitarians and their followers, the economists, aren't happy until they have translated a phenomenon into something recognizable on their familiar turf of individuals with preferences and constraints. But anthropologists are equally unhappy until they have translated those very same preferences into what is for them the familiar realm of culture. This difference makes it awkward to refer to the semantic view of explanation as reduction, which is the usual name for it in the philosophy of science. The word *reduction* seems to imply a hierarchy of explanation, in which "emergent" phenomena are "reduced" to "lower-level" ones. Such a view may make sense for the natural sciences, where it is common to think about reducing chemistry to physical chemistry and ultimately to physics. But it isn't very helpful in social science, where the final realms of the various disciplines and research traditions are not shared or ordered in any way.

The third view of explanation, as I noted, derives from the characteristics of explanation itself. Often we think an explanation is satisfactory simply because it is logically beautiful and compelling. Indeed, sometimes we find an explanation beautiful and satisfying without believing it at all. This is the reaction most people have to Freud on a first reading. It may or may not work, but how elegant it is! How simple yet comprehensive! Many have the same reaction to Jean Piaget's early work on the origins of intelligence in children. From such tiny postulates, he managed to produce so many insights! Reflective life creates in us a desire for pretty argument. We may not like its premises, its content, or its results, but we all appreciate its enticing mixture of complexity and clarity.[2]

Formal writing about explanation has usually taken this third view, that explanation has to do with the properties of an argument—specifically, its logical structure. In the most famous article on explanation in the twentieth century, the philosopher Carl Hempel argued that to explain is to demonstrate that the starting conditions in the case that we want to explain fit the hypothesis conditions of some general "covering law" (1942). For example, we might have the covering law that when a political party has a substantial majority in a parliament, it will be able to have a large effect on the country. Then we demonstrate in a particular case (say, Great Britain in 1997, after the Labour landslide) that one party had such a substantial majority. We can then say we have explained why the Labour Party has had a strong effect on British policies in the years after 1997: the conjunction of our covering law—"whenever a party has a strong majority, it has a big effect"—with our empirical premise—"Labour in 1997 got a strong majority"—logically entails the empirical conclusion that "Labour had a large effect on the country." By combining the general law with a demonstration that our particular case fits the condition of that law, we can use the conclusion of the law to explain the particular outcome in our particular case.

Hempel's view of explanation focused on the logical pattern of an account, on the way its parts are put together. His is a *syntactic* view of explanation, for it emphasizes the syntax of an account rather than its ability to help us act (the *pragmatic* view) or its ability to translate a phenomenon into a realm we think we understand intuitively (the *semantic* view).

Now the goal of social science, as I have said, is explanation of social life in whichever of these three senses we choose. A century or so of experience has taught social scientists some standard ways to go about this.[3]

II. METHODS

Social scientists have a number of methods, stylized ways of conducting their research that comprise routine and accepted procedures for doing the rigorous side of science. Each method is loosely attached to a community of social scientists for whom it is the right way to do things. But no method is the exclusive property of any one of the social sciences, nor is any social science, with the possible exception of anthropology, principally organized around the use of one particular method.[4]

One might expect that the various social science methods would be versions of a single explanatory enterprise or that they would be logical parts of some general scheme, but in practice they don't work that way. Far from being parts of a general scheme, they are somewhat separated from one another and often mutually hostile. In fact, many social scientists use methods that take for granted that other methods—used by other social scientists—are useless. But nobody cares much. The various methodological traditions roll along, happily ignoring one another most of the time.

It is therefore not at all obvious how best to classify methods. If we recall the basic questions of method—how to propose a question, how to design a study, how to draw inferences, how to acquire and analyze data—we can see that any one of these questions might be used to categorize methods. If we categorize by type of data gathering, there are four basic social science methods:

1. *ethnography:* gathering data by personal interaction
2. *surveys:* gathering data by submitting questionnaires to respondents or formally interviewing them
3. *record-based analysis:* gathering data from formal organizational records (censuses, accounts, publications, and so on)
4. *history:* using old records, surveys, and even ethnographies

If, by contrast, we begin with how one analyzes data, we might have three methods:

1. *direct interpretation:* analysis by an individual's reflection and synthesis (for example, narration)
2. *quantitative analysis:* analysis using one of the standard methods of statistics to reason about causes
3. *formal modeling:* analysis by creating a formal system mimicking the world and then using it to simulate reality

If we begin with how one poses a question, we might note the important issue of how many cases we consider. This would give us three kinds of methods:

1. *case-study analysis:* studying a unique example in great detail
2. *small-N analysis:* seeking similarities and contrasts in a small number of cases
3. *large-N analysis:* emphasizing generalizability by studying large numbers of cases, usually randomly selected

Any one of these categorizations could be used to classify methods. Moreover, putting these three category systems together gives one $4 \times 3 \times 3 = 36$ possible subtypes. And in fact, the majority of these subtypes have been tried by someone at some point or other.

Because there is no obvious list or categorization of methods, I will simply give five examples of conspicuously successful methodological traditions: ethnography, historical narration, standard causal analysis, small-N comparison, and formalization. Most of these have been hybridized in various ways, but we can look at the hybrids later if we need to. (Actually, small-N comparison will serve as an example of hybrid methods throughout.) Note that these five examples do not make up an exhaustive list. Indeed, they come out of different ways of categorizing methods. Ethnography is a way of gathering data, narration is a way of writing it up, small-N comparison is a choice of data size, standard causal analysis is a general analytic approach, and formalization is a specific analytic approach using purely abstract data. Let me reiterate. There is *no one basic way* to categorize methods, nor is there any simple set of dimensions for arraying them. Methodological traditions are like any other social phenomena. They are made by people working together, criticizing one another, and borrowing from other traditions. They are living social things, not abstract categories in a single system. Each of the five methods that follow is a living mode of inquiry with a long and distinguished lineage.

A. Ethnography

Ethnography means living inside the social situation one is studying and becoming to some extent a participant in it.

One's participation can range from mere observation to going native, from occasional afternoons to round-the-clock immersion. One can augment this participation with interviews, guidance from key informants, and review of official records.

An ethnographer's questions are often not very detailed before the field research begins, although the researcher will have a general puzzle or problem. As an ethnographer proceeds, he or she generates a mass of field notes: records of events, interviews, observations, and reflections about personal reactions, as well as endless verbatim records of conversations and interactions. The ethnographer floats into and out of the field situation, trying to keep an outsider's view even while developing an insider's one as well. Continually reading and rereading field notes, the ethnographer thinks up new questions to ask and new avenues to explore. This constant reflection is difficult, and as a result the field experience is disorienting, as is evident in the famous field diaries of the anthropologist Bronislaw Malinowski (1989).

When the fieldwork is done, the ethnographer returns home and contemplates these hundreds of pages of notes. Questions become clearer. Connections and themes begin to surface as the inchoate data are classified and reclassified, thought and rethought. The result is most often a monograph of some sort, with chapters that pose the now clear question, set the ethnographic scene, present extensive data from the field, and in the end provide a theoretical insight.

As an example, consider *Witchcraft, Oracles, and Magic among the Azande* by E. E. Evans-Pritchard. Evans-Pritchard made several extended sojourns among the Azande between 1926 and 1930. Interestingly, he did not go to the field to study what he eventually wrote about: "I had no interest in witchcraft when I went to Zandeland, but the Azande had; so I had to let myself be guided by them" (1976:242). As a result of that guidance, Evans-Pritchard wrote a monumental book that explores not only withcraft but all the "metaphysical" ideas of the remarkable Azande. The central question eventually became one of *why* the Azande held the beliefs they held about the supernatural and the nonobservable. Evans-Pritchard gave a functional answer to this question; beliefs in witchcraft, oracles, and magic served mainly to reinforce the social and cultural status quo. But this simplistic summary of the book belies its extraordinary richness. One comes away from it having questioned not only Azande beliefs but also one's own.

B. Historical Narration

Historical narration is another methodological tradition. Much of historical work is descriptive, examining the question of *what really was* the state of affairs in a particular place and time. But historians often pose a specific narrative question: most commonly, why did such and such an event take place? Historians apply many methods to such questions. Much of historical work consists of amassing published or archival materials from the time and place studied, so-called primary materials. Strange as it may seem, historical data are often embarrassingly rich; we often know too much about the details of the past. As a result, historical method often takes the form of trolling these seas of old data for important materials.

The heart of historical method is the reading of documents themselves. An informed historical reading of primary materials presupposes extensive—indeed overwhelming—knowledge of the time and place that produced them. Often this includes not only knowing the environing historical record but also knowing foreign languages (or old usages in one's own language) and indeed recognizing the historical and regional varieties both of languages and of the many forces behind the survival of the documents read. The historian (or any social scientist employing historical methods) walks a thin line between overinterpreting and underinterpreting sources. No source should be read out of context, but the art of historical discovery often lies in figuring out how previous conceptions of that context were wrong. Thus, reading documents *seems* easy but *is* difficult.

Like the ethnographer, the historian carries out many tasks simultaneously, now seeking documents, now reading them, now looking for more, now assembling preliminary arguments and recasting earlier interpretations. As with ethnography, there is a long and painstaking process by which a researcher assembles a synthetic view of something that is first perceived only through a welter of particular detail. But it has long been a custom of historians to hide their arduous research process under an elegant mantle of prose. Without question, history is the best written of the social sciences, perhaps the only social science that is read widely for pleasure by nonspecialists. As a result, history and in particular historical narrative seem at their best to be simple and effortless. That simplicity, however, is deceptive.

A classic example of historical work is A. J. P. Taylor's celebrated and contentious *Origins of the Second World War*. Taylor set himself the task of showing why the European war of 1939 broke out. One of the revolutionary aspects of Taylor's book was that it asked this question at all; previous writers had seen

Hitler's war as requiring no explanation. Taylor's materials included thousands of documents, memoirs, and published works in all the languages of Europe. As with most first-rate history, the methodological efforts that produced the book—the reading of this enormous mass of material, the interpretations tried and rejected, the sources sought but missed—disappear behind Taylor's smooth, ironic prose. His basic interpretation—that German foreign policy in the interwar period was brilliantly (and successfully) opportunistic and that Hitler's ingenuity deserted him only when he gratuitously invaded the Soviet Union and declared war on the United States—caused a furor for decades after its publication.

C. Standard Causal Analysis

Standard causal analysis (SCA) takes large numbers of cases, measures various aspects of them, and employs statistical models to draw inferences about the relationships among those measurements. It then uses the inferences to consider the causal factors that might have produced the correlational patterns that are observed in the data.

Causal analysis starts by defining a universe of cases in which it is interested. These can be anything: people, organizations, families, nations, cities. The cases are then measured by some common yardsticks. These variables can be unordered categories, like race, gender, graduate degree, occupation, or color of eyes. They can be ordered categories, like the familiar five-point attitude scale from "strongly disagree" to "disagree," "don't care," "agree," and "strongly agree." Or they can be continuous scales, like income, wealth, age, and level of education. Much of the hard work in standard causal analysis takes the form of finding, measuring, and assessing the distributions of these variables. As in ethnography and historical research, this apparently simple task of data gathering is easy to do badly if one is not careful.

One of the variables is taken, in each particular study, to be the dependent variable. That is, the analyst will seek to know the effects of all the other (independent) variables on this dependent one. Mathematically, the analyst tries to replace the dependent variable with a weighted sum of the independent variables. So if the dependent variable is income, for example, one takes so many parts education and so many parts occupation and so many parts gender, and so on, and sees how well one can predict income. There are many mathematical complexities to this approach, and there are several different ways of estimating the results, but the basic approach is always to vary the weights in order to find the weighted sum of the independent variables that *best predicts* the dependent variable. Note, however, that what is independent in one study can be dependent in another, and vice versa.

Analysts choose their variables by trying to think up causal stories that would imply that some variable has a powerful effect on another. Someone predicting individual racial attitudes will probably use region of birth as a predictor, for example. Note, too, that the mathematics does its best to control the interdependencies of the variables. *Either* education *or* occupation does pretty well predicting income by itself, but when the two are together, they aren't twice as good, because they are highly correlated with each other.

A classic example of this type of study is *The American Occupational Structure* by Peter Blau and Otis Dudley Duncan. In this great work, Blau and Duncan wanted to understand the forces that determine the kinds of occupations people end up in. They were particularly concerned with the degree to which parents' occupations influenced their children's occupations. Twenty thousand male respondents filled out a questionnaire on many topics, among them their race, their occupation and education, and their parents' occupation, education, and employment. The occupations were not treated as categories (doctor, lawyer, and so on) but were converted to a single continuous prestige scale. Thus, the actual dependent variable was the *prestige* of the occupation held by the respondent at the time of the survey (1962). In their basic model, Blau and Duncan showed that the most important factors in determining a respondent's current job status were his educational level and the status of his first job (since the men were of widely varying ages, some had had many jobs). Nearly all the effects of respondent's *father's* education and job came through these two "intervening" variables. (That is, father's education and father's occupation affected respondent's education and first job, which in turn affected the respondent's job as of 1962.) The Blau and Duncan study, which of course had dozens of other findings, helped inaugurate two decades of research on this process of "occupational status attainment."

D. *Small-N Comparison*

Partway between the detailed analysis of the historical or current reality of a single case and the statistical analysis of many cases lies a method we can call small-N comparison. Typically, small-N comparison investigates a handful of cases, from three to perhaps a dozen. The cases can be many different kinds of things: bureaucracies, nations, social service agencies, communities, or any other form of social organization.

The particular form of data gathering employed in small-N analysis can vary. There are ethnographies comparing several different field sites as well as histories comparing several different trajectories of nations or classes. Small-N analysis typically emerges within ethnographic and historical traditions and is usually seen as a way of improving generalizations by invoking more (and different) cases. It occasionally arises from the reverse process, in which a quantitative analyst focuses on a small number of cases to improve his or her "reading" of the variables.[5]

Small-N comparison attempts to combine the advantages of single-case analysis with those of multicase analysis, at the same time trying to avoid the disadvantages of each. On the one hand, it retains much information about each case. On the other, it compares the different cases to test arguments in ways that are impossible with a single case. By making these detailed comparisons, it tries to avoid the standard criticism of single-case analysis—that one can't generalize from a single case—as well as the standard criticism of multicase analysis— that it oversimplifies and changes the meaning of variables by removing them from their context.

Small-N analysis has been characteristic of a number of areas in social science. The field of comparative politics has been built on small-N comparison, as has historical sociology. In both cases, there is heavy reliance on secondary literatures concerning the individual cases. Most anthropologists, by contrast, have gone directly from single-case analysis to abstract generalizations based on categorization of dozens of cases (for example, in studies of kinship, totemism, or folklore), although anthropological linguists have often used comparisons of relatively small numbers of cases.

A classic example of small-N analysis is Barrington Moore's *Social Origins of Dictatorship and Democracy*. This book compares routes to modernity in England, France, the United States, China, Japan, and India. Germany and Russia are also considered, but not in depth. Moore's sources included hundreds of histories of this or that aspect of each country. After endless reading, comparison, and reflection, Moore theorized three basic routes to modernity, all of them depending on how the traditional agricultural classes—lords and peasants—dealt with the coming of commercial agriculture and the rise of the bourgeoisie. In the first route, that of England, France, and the United States, a powerful commercial middle class overthrew the landed classes or forced them to accept middle-class terms. The result was democracy. In Germany and Japan, the bourgeois revolution failed, and the landed classes determined the shape and dynamics of capitalism as it emerged, leading to fascism. In China and Russia, an enormous peasant class provided the main force behind revolution, thus undercutting the drive to capitalism and leading to a standoff between the revolutionaries in the advanced capitalist sector (the Communists) and the peasants. Moore's book provided the stimulus for much of comparative politics and historical sociology in the 1970s, 1980s, and 1990s.

E. Formalization

There are methods in social science that work without much data at all. Or rather they work with what are called stylized facts. These methods are not methods in the usual sense but rather modes of reasoning about social reality that require some "quasi-factual" input. They are thus halfway between theories and methods.

A good example of this kind of formalization is analysis of the life table. A life table is a description of what happens to a cohort (traditionally, 100,000 individuals) after n years of life: how many are still living, what number and percentage died that year, what the expectation of life is for those remaining, and so on. By combining life tables with birth-rate information, we can work out age distributions for a population, investigate the structure of generations, predict future family structure, and make many other useful demographic projections. We haven't gathered new information but have simply worked out the details implied by the information we already have.

Formalization has gone furthest, of course, in economics, where it has sometimes lost contact with social reality altogether. But formal thinking is important throughout social science. The great anthropologist Claude Lévi-Strauss attempted a largely formal analysis of myths, breaking myths up into a linear, narrative dimension on the one hand and a timeless, structural dimension on the other (1967). The sociologist Harrison White treated job markets (like those for clergymen and college presidents) as if they were electron-hole systems, in which vacancies rather than moving people had the initiative (1970). Mathematical geographers treat arrangements of political boundaries as if they were the product of universal mathematical relationships (Haggett, Cliff, and Frey 1977).

More than any other methodological tradition, formalization lives by borrowing. By nature, formalization is portable, and many a formal analyst has made a reputation by borrowing. Economists borrowed much of their formalism from thermodynamics. Sociologists have borrowed formalisms from physics and biology.

A good example of formalization is Thomas Schelling's famous model of segregation, originally published in 1971 and republished in his remarkable *Micromotives and Macrobehavior*. The Schelling model presumes two kinds of people, one much more numerous than the other, and a neighborhood that people of both kinds would like to live in. Both groups have a similar "tolerance distribution," which describes how willing they are to live in communities of varying mixes of the two populations. The most tolerant within each group will live in a neighborhood as a one-third minority, while the least tolerant will live only in a totally segregated neighborhood, all of their own kind. Under these conditions, Schelling shows, the only two stable equilibriums for the particular neighborhood considered are the fully segregated ones. He goes on to demonstrate that if the two groups were of equal size and if the most tolerant of each group were a little more tolerant, there would be a stable fifty-fifty equilibrium. He also shows that if the larger group included *more intolerant* people, there would be a stable integrated equilibrium (because people from the larger group wouldn't keep moving into the neighborhood, frightening out the less tolerant members of the smaller group).

The Schelling models require no real data, only stylized data. But they tell us something important and counterintuitive. They tell us that even somewhat tolerant populations have a hard time producing integrated neighborhoods when the populations vastly differ in size and indeed that sometimes more tolerance leads to more segregation.[6]

ETHNOGRAPHY, historical narration, standard causal analysis, small-N analysis, and formalization are thus five examples of reasonably successful methodological traditions. Each has its style and its proponents. Each has been combined with these and other methods in a bewildering variety of ways. I want to reiterate that these methodological traditions are not associated *absolutely* with any discipline, although ethnography and narration are somewhat associated with anthropology and history, respectively. I also want to reiterate that these methods do not follow from a single mode of categorization of methods. As I noted, some are methods of analysis, some are ways of gathering data, and so on. They are, if anything, best thought of as practices, as ways of doing social science. As such, they are produced by communities of researchers who practice them, teach them, and develop them. They are living traditions, not abstract recipes.

III. EXPLANATORY PROGRAMS

You may be wondering when you would use one of these methods as opposed to another. Are there hypotheses or empirical problems particularly well suited to particular methods? The usual answer to this question is yes, and the usual procedure would be to present here a list of what method is good for what kind of problem. But my answer to the question of suitability is no. I don't think there are methods that are particularly good for particular questions. So I have no such list. Rather, I will show that the different methods are in fact aiming to do different things; they envision different kinds of explanations. That argument takes up the rest of this chapter. Chapter Two then shows how the standard idea of "well-suited methods" rests on false assumptions about the methods, and as a result suitability falls apart as a concept. The good news is that that falling apart creates important openings for heuristics, which are, after all, what we are looking for.

We begin by seeing how different methods are in fact trying to accomplish different things. We do this by putting sections I and II of the chapter together, relating the methods just discussed to the three broad senses of explanation introduced earlier.

Each of the three senses of explanation defines an *explanatory program*, a general style of thinking about questions of explanation. And each explanatory program has some versions that are more concrete and some versions that are more abstract. With three explanatory programs, each having concrete and abstract versions, there are six total possibilities. To give the whole analysis in simple form ahead of time:

1. Ethnography is a *concrete* version of the *semantic* explanatory program.
2. Historical narration is a *concrete* version of the *syntactic* explanatory program.
3. Formalization is an *abstract* version of the *syntactic* explanatory program.
4. SCA is an *abstract* version of the *pragmatic* explanatory program.

Note that there are two missing possibilities. I shall say very little about one of them: the *concrete* version of the *pragmatic* program. Think of this as simple experimentation, something we don't do much of in social science unless you think of psychology—which involves a lot of experiments—as a social science. I shall say more about the other missing cell: the *abstract* version of the *semantic* program. Although it has no single name, this is probably the most rapidly evolving area of methods in the social sciences.

This analysis can be seen visually in the figure on page 29. The three dimensions are the three types of explanations. For each of these, the origin stands for explanations focused on everyday particulars, on commonsense events. These are an anchor for each explanatory program, rooting it in the everyday world. From this base, "universalizing" moves reach from the origin toward abstraction along each of the principal axes of explanation. The *syntactic* program explains the social world by more and more abstractly *modeling* its particular action and interrelationships. The *semantic* program explains the world of social particulars by assimilating it to more and more general *patterns*, searching for regularities over time or across social space. Finally, the purely *pragmatic* program tries to separate more and more clearly the effects of different potential interventions or *causes* from one another.

The reader should *not* read this little exercise as a definitive classification of methods but rather as a way to see that the various methods are in many ways trying to do different kinds of things. In particular, I am *not* assuming, as much of empirical social science does, that all explanation involves thinking about causality. We should separate the concept of explanation from that of understanding the causes of something. Our notion of understanding the causes of things has become very narrow in social science, in contrast to the much more general idea of causality that obtains, for example, in the law.

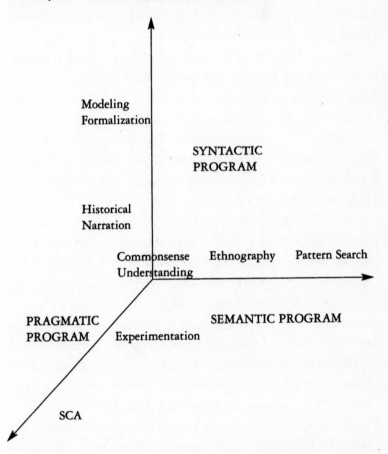

Let me now show in more detail how this argument works. We start with the programs relating to particulars: concrete, real events rather than abstract ones. Ethnography exemplifies *semantic* explanation of particular events, while historical narration exemplifies *syntactic* explanation of particular events. Both are found near the origin of the figure above, but they lie on different dimensions. This is not because of their difference in temporality but because of their difference in general explanatory style: translation-semantic type on the one hand, narrative-syntactic type on the other.

A brief aside about temporality. Temporality is a particularly important issue in explanation. Some explanations are focused on processes, on the embedding of social life in moving time. Others devote most of their attention to complex interrelationships in a static "present"; they think social life takes place within a given structure, which they treat as fixed for the time being.[7] It is important to recognize that *all* explanatory programs have temporal and atemporal versions. For example, there are temporal versions of history (narrative histories like Thucydides' *History of the Peloponnesian War*) and atemporal ones (descriptions of a moment, like Sir Lewis Namier's *Structure of Politics at the Accession of George III*). Temporality is another dimension I could have used to classify methods, but I prefer to leave it for later chapters because of the importance of time in heuristics. What must be emphasized here is that temporality is *not* one of the dimensions that differentiates types of explanations or explanatory programs more broadly. All explanations have to think about time in one way or another.

Returning then to the main argument. In ethnography, the act of explanation is chiefly semantic. When we say that Malinowski, in his great *Argonauts of the Western Pacific*, has explained why the Trobrianders paddle around the islands giving and receiving shells, what we mean is that he has told us enough about their culture and their social life that we can understand why they would do this. We can envision what it is that they see themselves doing, and we can see what they are doing as reasonable, as something we would do if we were in their place. The field-worker has translated, however imperfectly, their world into one that we find comprehensible. Typically, ethnography accomplishes this by providing detail, by showing ramifications, and by embedding the strange habits of unfamiliar people in the everyday habits of those same people and then connecting their everyday world with our own. The ethnographer may have other professional aims, of course. To return to an earlier example, Evans-Pritchard takes pains, in *Witchcraft, Oracles, and Magic*, to explain to us that the idea of witchcraft serves the epistemological and social function of explaining unfortunate events, an argument by which he sets forth his functional theory of culture. But the *explanation* of witchcraft lies less in the syntax of functionalist explanation than in Evans-Pritchard's ability to translate the activities of the Azande into something thinkable by Western minds. Evans-Pritchard does this semantic translation, for example, in his offhand remark about using the Azande poison oracles to run his everyday life. The Azande make daily decisions by posing a yes-or-no question (for example, should I do ethnography today or not?) while feeding young chickens a small dose of poison. A chicken then makes the decision by living (yes) or dying (no):

> I always kept a supply of poison for the use of my household
> and neighbours and we regulated our affairs in accordance
> with the oracles' decisions. I may remark that I found this as
> satisfactory a way of running my home and affairs as any other
> I know of. (1976:126)

It is not Evans-Pritchard's functional theory that persuades, but this homey detail. *Witchcraft, Oracles, and Magic* is an explanatory success because of its semantic virtues, not its syntactic ones.

Of course, ethnography can have pragmatic and syntactic virtues as well. Ethnography of the drug culture is probably our only effective means to pragmatic intervention in that culture. And Lévi-Strauss's structural anthropology had as its chief virtue an extraordinary syntactic elegance that sometimes amounted to a kind of monomania. But the deep virtue of ethnography as an explanatory program lies in translation. It is principally a semantic program.

By contrast, the great virtue of *narrative* explanation lies in *syntax*. The longstanding literature on the philosophy of history is clear on this point. When Alexis de Tocqueville tells us, in *The Old Régime and the French Revolution*, why that revolution came about, he may here and there employ general laws about social life. But the reason we think his book explains the revolution is that he tells a followable, reasonable story in which a particular sequence of events under those general laws leads in some inevitable way to the revolution. We don't notice his assumptions of general causal laws (for example, "people with large amounts of power don't give it away"). What we notice is the sweeping story that draws us along with France into the maelstrom of revolution.

This syntactic strength is, of course, by no means an abstract one. Narration seems persuasive precisely because telling stories is how we explain most things in daily life. To be sure, there are some quite abstract narrative concepts: evolution (in Herbert Spencer's sociology), habituation (in Max Weber's sociology and throughout psychology), dialectical conflict (in Marxian social analysis), and the like. But these are for scholars.

The real reason we feel that historical narration explains is that narration is the syntax of commonsense explanation, the one we use all the time ourselves. So there is no need to justify it. Indeed, the analytical philosophers of history never could really demonstrate *how* narration explains; they just said over and over that it does.

Like ethnography, narration has other explanatory virtues. Narration often moves us toward a simpler semantic plane. The narrative ideals of followability (Gallie 1968) and reenactment (Collingwood 1946) follow the same semantic principles as ethnography. They measure a narrative's ability to locate us as reasonable persons within itself, as people who *would* have done what *was* done had we been the actors of whom we read. And narration can also have pragmatic virtues. Often, the first step to undertaking action in any particular situation is developing a narrative of how it got to be the way that it is. But again, neither of these is a basic virtue. Serious narration explains things for us because we use unserious narration all day every day. Narration is the syntax of everyday understanding.

The explanatory programs illustrated by both ethnography and narration thus appeal to the commonsense world; the first appeals to the commonsense *content* of everyday experience, the second to the basic explanatory *syntax* of everyday life. Two major streams of explanatory practice in social science grow out of moves to make these two programs more abstract and formal. (This means moving away from the origin in the figure on page 29.) On the one hand, we have the attempt to formalize explanatory *syntax* in modeling and simulation, which embody what I will here call the syntactic explanatory program. This is the explanatory practice that is the *abstract* version of what *narration* is at the concrete level. On the other hand, we have the equivalent effort to formalize *semantics*, embodied in the family of techniques loosely known as data reduction and pattern search. This strand is the *abstract* version of what *ethnography* is at the concrete level; I shall call it the semantic explanatory program. (It is the important omitted cell mentioned a few pages back, pattern search in its most general version.)

Formal modeling and simulation embody the attempt (atemporal in formal modeling and temporal in simulation) to improve *syntactic* explanation by making it more abstract. The crucial quality sought in the syntactic explanatory program is elegance. In it, a set of statements "explain" some phenomenon if they offer a rigorous, complex, yet simple formal representation of it. On the atemporal side, there are many embodiments of this program: game theory, classical microeconomics, the Markovian tradition in social mobility analysis, the group theoretic version of network theory. The temporal side—expressed most clearly in simulation—has had fewer adherents in social science, although Jay Forrester gave it a very public demonstration in his studies of industrial, urban, and world dynamics in the 1960s, and it has returned in the guise of simulation games. These various methods are astonishingly elegant, some in their mathematics, some in their simplicity, some in their ability to produce unexpected results, some in their extraordinary coherence. All are clear, parsimonious, and in a deep way intellectually pleasing to the abstract mind.

At the same time, these methods share a breathtaking disattention to semantics, to the reference from model to reality. This is well shown by the diversity of some models' applications. Microeconomics was systematized by Irving Fisher (in the early twentieth century) by borrowing whole cloth the methods of statistical thermodynamics, as if gases and people behaved in the same way. Group theory (a particular branch of modern algebra) saw major application in crystallography and in pure mathematics as well as in sociology's network theory and even anthropology's kinship analysis. Game theory has journeyed from psychological experiments to explaining the stock market and modeling family-planning decisions. Of course, proponents of the syntactic program argue that semantics in fact doesn't matter. These empirical realities all have the same general semantic form, they say, and so one can write abstract syntax for them.

But most readers find the *semantic* assumptions of the syntactic program quite worrisome. What is the point of game-theory models if we can write ten different models for any given social situation? We must choose between those models on semantic grounds, and about those semantic grounds the syntactic program tells us nothing. What is the point of admiring the elegance of microeconomics if microeconomics frankly admits that preferences cannot be generated from inside the system without undercutting the assumptions of the whole edifice? Essentially, microeconomics is telling us that if we can explain what people want to do, *it* can then explain that they do it. So what?

In summary, the syntactic program buys elegance and breadth at the price of semantic indeterminacy and limitation. By contrast with this syntactic explanation via elegant and highly general arguments, the *semantic* program seeks to explain social reality by a different kind of abstraction. It directly simplifies the complexity of the social world, turning it into a reduced description that a reasonable reader can grasp with the *syntax* of everyday explanation. Thus, techniques like cluster analysis and multidimensional scaling take data of enormous detail and turn it into simple categories and pictures. Pierre Bourdieu, for example, "explained" consumption patterns in France (in his book *Distinction*) by showing that those patterns constitute a language of class distinctions. From the reader's point of view, the explanation is a matter of common sense once Bourdieu has visually presented the "geometry" of the consumption patterns by using a scaling technique that turns raw data on people's preferences for cultural materials into a picture locating types of goods and types of people on the same map.

The semantic program has been strong in psychology and particularly strong in market research; marketers routinely use cluster analysis to reduce the American consumer market to one hundred or so basic types of consumers. In that sense, the semantic program has shown considerable pragmatic strength as well. (These are the techniques that are used to figure out your consumption preferences from your Internet use, for example.) On the syntactic side, however, the semantic program has been weak. Its overwhelming focus on one-time analysis makes it static. It can abstractly describe a state of affairs but cannot account for how it changes. Network analysis is one of the glories of abstract semantic explanation, but there is still no real conceptualization for the temporal development of networks. Only when some researchers recently began to think about applying pattern search techniques to over-time data did any kind of syntactic development arrive in the semantic program. In short, as with the syntactic program, power of one type was bought at the price of indeterminacy of the other.

I have so far described concrete and abstract versions of the syntatic program (history and formal modeling, respectively) and concrete and abstract versions of the semantic program (ethnography and pattern search, respectively). There is a third abstracting move in social scientific explanation, the one that moves out from the origin along the *pragmatic* dimension of the figure on page 29. Oddly enough, this program has become so successful that social scientists have forgotten that pragmatics is its origin. This is the program carried out by the standard forms of causal analysis in social science, both analysis of the cross-sectional type (as in structural equations models or path analysis) and of the temporal type (as in durational models). Because the SCA program is so dominant in empirical social science, we need to look at it in some detail.

The SCA paradigm arose out of a rationalization of the methods it uses, methods that were originally used to interpret practical experiments. As we saw earlier, these methods work by taking apart the complex particulars in the data (the cases) and treating them as intersections of abstract, universal properties (the variables). Analysis then isolates one of those variables—an arbitrarily chosen dependent variable—and searches out the effects of the other, so-called independent variables on it. Interaction effects—that is, effects arising from two or more variables "working together"—are treated as secondary.

The great explanatory virtue of this method, as originally conceived, was pragmatic. Sir Ronald Fisher and his followers devised these statistical techniques in the 1920s and 1930s to test the effects of experimental manipulations. Should one add fertilizer or not? Was soil A better than soil B? They put the fertilizer on some fields but not others, measured the effects, and figured out a probability theory for the resulting numbers. They had no particular concern for causes, for why or how growth happened. The point was to decide whether to take some action, not to understand mechanisms. Since the original applications were experimental, these statistical techniques were in fact explanatorily quite persuasive for the pragmatic purpose they served. Used in an experimental context—as they still often are in psychology—they remain so.

Later in the century, however, this approach was applied to nonexperimental data and combined with new ideas about causality. This led to the hybrid explanatory program that is now general throughout the empirical social sciences, the standard causal analysis program. The SCA program still has some pragmatic relevance; the methods are still used in evaluation research, for example. But its main uses are not now pragmatic. Rather, they pretend to be syntactic. So we say (using the weighted-sums approach mentioned earlier) that differences in wages in civil service systems are "caused by" gender, bureaucracy, unionization, and so on. *Semantically*, of course, this whole language of variables is a mirage. The words *gender* and *bureaucracy* do not refer to real entities. Gender and bureaucracy do not exist as independent things; they exist only as *properties* of real things (in this case, of civil service systems). So this "properties" syntax has to be justified by further *semantic* reference. We have to have some way to give empirical meaning to statements about relationships between abstract things like gender and bureaucracy. In economics, this semantic reference is made to formal and simplified models of action. So typical economics articles in the SCA tradition justify their SCA with a mass of formalizing and calculus that typically begins each article. In sociology and political science, this external reference is made to a set of simplified narratives. So sociology and political science articles of the SCA type begin not with the calculus of the economists but with commonsense historical narratives of the form "such and such people are likely to do such and such things under such and such conditions." These stories try to justify the "variables-level syntax" by reaching toward the semantic world of everyday reasonable understanding. Thus, in order to be explanatory, the SCA program has to combine its variables-level causal *syntax* with unrelated *semantic* references to other, more credible syntactic approaches to reality: stylized action in the economics case, followable narratives in the sociology one.

All of this complexity happens because in reality the SCA program has no causal foundation at all; it was originally designed to help us make decisions, to be pragmatic. Dressed up as a syntactic program, it is ungracious and silly. (It is also surprisingly difficult to learn, since its rationale—as this long discussion shows—is quite tortured.) Its strongest point remains its ability to tell us about the comparative size of variables' pragmatic effects on other variables, given the implicit assumption that we have a quasi-experimental situation (which we almost never do). But it can't even tell us in which direction the causal forces work nor how causes work together. All of those judgments must be imported from elsewhere.[8]

In summary, there is no free lunch. Strongly developing any one aspect of explanation ends up losing much of the rest. In particular, the present moment in social science is probably one in which the syntactic and semantic programs are about to turn the tables on the pragmatic one, which has dominated social science for about sixty years. The latter remains the best program when we think about social policy. But if we are trying to understand why and how things happen, it has little to recommend it.

Chapter Two

Basic Debates and Methodological Practices

The preceding chapter located standard methods in larger explanatory programs directed at understanding social life. In this chapter, I turn to the more traditional understanding of these methods, according to which they embody certain assumptions about science and social life. The chapter first discusses the principal debates about these assumptions. It then locates the methods of Chapter One with respect to these major debates.

It is here that the argument leaves the standard path. The customary text would at this point go on to a chapter-length analysis of the details of each method. Many excellent texts do so. Instead, I will show that on closer inspection, the usual, simple picture of the methods comes apart in our hands. In the first place, *each* method offers a profound critique of *each* of the others, critiques that are aligned along quite different dimensions. As a result, the various methodological critiques can be arranged in tail-chasing circles. They do not offer the single choice that they are usually said to embody (quantitative versus qualitative, science versus interpretation, or something like that). This circular quality guarantees an openness, a heuristic richness, to mutual methodological critiques. And in the second place, the great debates themselves prove to have a fractal character; they repeat themselves again and again at finer and finer levels within the methods. As a result, they too function less as fixed positions than as methodological resources, as gambits of invention and discovery. Later in the book (Chapter Six), I will show that these debates are in fact our richest resources for new ideas.

I. BASIC DEBATES

Chapter One showed how methods can be loosely identified with different programs of explanation. But it is more common to look at methods in terms of their positions on certain basic social science debates. I shall list nine such debates.

A. Positivism and Interpretivism

The first two debates concern methodology proper. One strand of social science argues that social life can be measured. These measures are independent of context, replicable by different people, and comparable for accuracy and validity. By contrast, another strand of social science holds that measurement of social life is not possible or—what is the same thing—that the things that can be measured are unimportant or meaningless. Events that seem to be measurable in fact acquire meaning only when it is assigned to them in interaction. Hence, there can be no decontextualized, universal measure.

This opposition is quite drastic. For the first group, social research takes the form of measurement and counting. For the second, it takes the form of interaction and interpretation. These two positions are called *positivism* and *interpretivism*.

B. Analysis and Narration

A second deep debate in social science—one already apparent in the preceding chapter—concerns types of analysis. Many social scientists think that telling a story is a sufficient account of something. For them, narration can explain. By contrast, many others believe that only some more abstract analysis can explain something. Usually the latter position emphasizes causality. To tell why something happens, in this view, is not to tell a story about it but rather to list the various effects *individual* forces have on it "net of other things": what is the effect of race on income? of education on occupation? and so on. This second debate pits *narration* against *analysis*.

These two debates—positivism/interpretivism and narration/ analysis—are easily stated. But it would be hard to overestimate their importance. They are utterly pervasive in the social sciences. Probably the majority of methodological reflection addresses them in one way or another.

These first two debates concern issues of method proper. But debates about the nature of social reality itself—debates about social ontology—also have important implications for methods, and so we shall consider them as well.

C. *Behaviorism and Culturalism*

A first ontological debate concerns analytic realms. Many social scientists draw a distinction between social structure and culture. Loosely speaking, *social structure* refers to regular, routine patterns of behavior. Demographic phenomena are perhaps the best example. The processes of birth, death, marriage, and migration seem to have a regularity all their own. One can discuss the demographic life and future of a population without much reference to phenomena outside demography or even to the "meaning" of demographic events themselves. By contrast, one would hardly think about the development of language or of religion in such behavioral terms. Language and religion are *cultural* systems, systems of symbols by which people understand and direct their lives; one cannot ignore their meanings.

The analytic distinction between social structure and culture has an obvious methodological avatar. The methodological position of *behaviorism* rejects any concern with culture and meaning. One can consider only social structure and behavior, not meaning. There is no standard name for the opposite position, which I shall call *culturalism*. On this position, social life is incomprehensible without investigation of the symbolic systems that index and encode it. The behaviorism/culturalism debate is obviously close to the positivism/interpretivism one. But as with all of these distinctions, it is useful to cross the two and see what comes out. Suppose one were a positivist and a culturalist. That would mean that one was committed to the study of cultural phenomena but with positivist methods. Indeed, such scholars exist: anthropologists who measure and count the various meanings of category systems among primitive peoples, for example.

D. *Individualism and Emergentism*

A second debate about the nature of the social world—another that we have already encountered—is the debate over individuals and emergents. Certain social scientists believe as a matter of principle that the only real entities in the social world are human individuals. All activity is done by human individuals, and anything that appears to be "emergent" (social) behavior must be the merely accidental result of individual processes. This program of *methodological individualism* goes back historically to the notion that the interaction of individual self-interests produces the social world we observe, an idea that first emerged full-blown in the early eighteenth century with Bernard Mandeville's *Fable of the Bees*. As a general scientific program, methodological individualism is even older, looking back to the long scientific heritage of atomism, with its concept of a universe built by combining little units.

Emergentists disagree. For them, the social is real. In more recent social thought, it was Émile Durkheim who argued most strongly for the explicit reality of social level. His famous book *Suicide* used the astonishing stability of suicide rates over time in particular countries and particular populations to demonstrate the existence of social forces irreducible to combinations of individual events. In practice, emergentist assumptions are quite common in social science methods. There may be many social scientists who deny the existence of Marxian-type classes, but there are few who deny the existence of occupations as social groups or the reality of commercial firms as social actors.

E. Realism and Constructionism

A third ontological debate concerns the question of whether the things and qualities we encounter in social reality are enduring phenomena or simply produced (or reproduced) in social interaction as need be. If we ask survey respondents to tell us about their ethnicity, for example, we may simply be encouraging them to invent an answer. In their everyday life, they may not think of themselves as ethnic. Or consider homosexuality. We know from national data that far more men and women have had sexual experiences with members of their own sex than think they are homosexual. If we ask about experience, we get one figure; if we ask about identity, we get one much smaller. That being true, can we in fact determine sexual identity with a questionnaire, or is it revealed only in interaction?

Here again we have two positions, in this case *realism* and *constructionism*. According to the first, the social process is made up of well-defined people and groups doing well-understood things in specifiable environments. According to the second, the social process is made up of people who construct their identities and selves in the process of interaction with one another; they and their activities have no meaning outside the flow of interaction itself. In this second view, people become ethnic (sometimes) when they are in interactions that call on them to be so: when challenged by others with strong ethnic identities, when ethnic identity might be materially rewarded, and so on. Otherwise, many of them may not be ethnic in any sense. The same argument might apply to homosexuality.

F. Contextualism and Noncontextualism

The distinction between realism and constructionism (or as it is sometimes called, objective and subjective views of social reality) overlaps another one, between thinking *contextually* and thinking *noncontextually*. In the contextual mode of approaching social life, a social statement or action has no meaning unless we know the context in which it appeared. If I say I am a political liberal, my statement has no real content until you know with whom I am comparing myself. I could be a middle-of-the-road Republican speaking to a member of the new Christian right, or I could be a left-wing Democrat comparing myself with all Republicans. Or again, if I say a community is disorganized, I could mean not that it is disorganized in some abstract sense but that it is disorganized relative to other communities around it. Note that the latter statement is not only a statement about the state of a community but also potentially a predictive statement about causal affairs. A community may attract certain kinds of people *because* it is disorganized relative to its surrounding communities, whereas it might be *losing* precisely those kinds of people if it were surrounded by a different set of communities. From this point of view, there is no absolute scale of disorganization, only disorganization relative to a context. In the noncontextual mode, by contrast, the meaning of disorganization or liberalism is the same no matter what. Obviously, the assumption of such noncontextuality is central to survey methods. When we send out questionnaires, we are assuming that everyone who answers has the same frame of reference in mind.[1]

THERE ARE THUS several important debates about the nature of social reality that have methodological implications. The first involves the analytic distinction between social and cultural realms, with its associated methodological schemes of behaviorism and culturalism. A second, long-standing debate is between individualism and emergentism, with its associated schemes of methodological individualism and methodological emergentism. Third is the pairing of realism and constructionism, and fourth is its closely related cousin pairing of contextualism and noncontextualism. Each of these debates has important implications for methodological positions.

G. Choice and Constraint
Not all of the basic social scientific debates concern methods or ontology, however. Some of them concern the kinds of things that are to be explained, what is taken to be problematic in social life. A first issue is whether to focus on *choice* or *constraint*. In many ways, this is another version of the individualism/emergentism debate. For economists in particular, the key to

understanding society lies in understanding how people make choices or rather in figuring out the consequences of their making choices in groups. (Economists feel they already know how people make choices—by maximizing utility subject to a budget constraint. The question lies in figuring out how they make those choices and what the social consequences are when groups of people make such decisions in parallel.)

For many other social scientists, however, the key to understanding society is in figuring out—as the economist James Duesenberry once famously put it—"why people have no choices to make" (1960:233). On this view, social structure constrains and directs individuals. They are not free to make their way unconstrained, except in specifically designed institutional structures like economic markets. Rather, they are shaped by social forces, arrangements and connections that prevent free choice from exercising anything like a determinant role.

H. Conflict and Consensus

Another long-standing debate concerns *conflict* and *consensus*. The consensus position is that while people are inherently disorderly and social order is therefore precarious, social organization and institutions keep people from destroying themselves. (The reader may recognize this position as descending from the English philosopher Thomas Hobbes.) For this position, the standard question is why conflict does not pervade the social system. The answer is usually sought in norms, rules, and values—all the apparatus of social institutions, as this position calls them. Much of consensus research takes the form of teasing out hidden norms and rules that maintain stability in social situations, from the grand social values seen by writers like

Talcott Parsons to the petty regulations of interaction rituals seen by writers like Erving Goffman.

The conflict position, with a genealogy reaching back through Marx to Rousseau, is precisely the reverse. Why, conflict theorists ask, is there so *much* conflict? The answer is that while people are inherently good, their lives are clouded by oppressive institutions that make them act in socially destructive ways. Conflict theorists also seek hidden norms and rules, but for them these are the concealed sources of conflict, not the visible bulwarks against it. Conflict thinkers always begin with social conflict and look backward for its causes, since they believe these do not lie in human nature. Consensus theorists think from conflict forward, to its consequences, believing as they do that conflict does arise in human nature.

In the area of problematics, then, we have two important debates: choice/constraint and conflict/consensus. It should be obvious that the conflict and consensus positions have distinct political sympathies, conflict with left-liberal thinking and consensus with conservative thinking. (Constraint and choice often follow the same divide.) These political positions themselves are often linked to a further debate, one on the nature of knowledge.

I. Transcendent and Situated Knowledge
Much of social science strains toward knowledge that applies at all times and in all places. This is the traditional "scientific" position in favor of *transcendent*, or *universal*, knowledge. An equally strong strain holds that such knowledge is not possible. Knowledge is always *situated*. The latter argument often rests on the constructionist position that social life is built in action

and hence that only the participants can correctly define what is happening in their own place and time. They have privileged access to their own reality. (This is certainly a position that even quite a few survey analysts would accept.)

The political sympathies of these positions are by no means consistent. The universalist, or transcendent, position is usually portrayed as politically conservative, while the left is identified with situated knowledge that accepts the limits of place and time. At the same time, much of left-liberal social science consists of applying universal moral positions (for example, "oppression is bad") to places and times that would by no means have accepted them. The connection is thus not consistent.

THE TRANSCENDENT/SITUATED KNOWLEDGE DEBATE is a useful place to complete this short survey of profound debates in social science. As we have seen, these begin with purely methodological debates: positivism/interpretivism and analysis/narration. They continue through the debates rooted in ontology: behaviorism/culturalism, individualism/emergentism, realism/constructionism, and contextualism/noncontextualism. To these are added the great debates over problematics: choice/constraint and conflict/consensus. Finally, as we have just noted, the characterization of the social sciences as transcendent or situated captures a host of differences about the sources and status of social scientific knowledge. I have listed all of these debates schematically in Table 2.1.

Table 2.1

THE BASIC DEBATES

Methodological Debates

- *Positivism*: reality is measurable.
- *Interpretivism*: there is no meaning without interaction and hence no measurement in the abstract.

- *Analysis*: there is no explanation without causality.
- *Narration*: stories can explain.

Debates about Social Ontology

- *Behaviorism*: social structure (i.e., routine behabvior) is the proper foundation of analysis.
- *Culturalism*: culture (i.e., symbolic systems) is the proper foundation for analysis.

- *Individualism*: Human individuals and their acts are the only real objects of social scientific analysis.
- *Emergentism*: social emergents exist, are irreducible to individuals, and can be real objects of social scientific analysis.

- *Realism*: social phenomena have endurance and stability; analysis should focus on the enduring, stable qualities of social phenomena.
- *Constructionism*: social phenomena are continually reproduced in interaction; analysis should focus on that reproduction.

- *Contextualism*: social phenomena are inevitably contextual and cannot be analyzed without taking account of context.
- *Noncontextualism*: social phenomena have meaning (and can be analyzed) independent of their contexts.

Debates about Problematics

- *Choice*: analysis should focus on why and how actors make choices and on the consequences of those choices.
- *Constraint*: analysis should focus on the structural constraints that govern action.

- *Conflict*: we need to explain why there is so much social conflict.
- *Consensus*: we need to explain why there is not more social conflict.

Debate about Types of Knowledge

- *Transcendent knowledge*: our knowledge should apply at all places and times. It should be "universal."
- *Situated knowledge*: our knowledge must be limited in its application. It is always local or particular.

II. METHODS AND DEBATES

The most common way of characterizing the methods introduced in Chapter One is by defining them not as flexible explanatory programs (as I did in that chapter), but in terms of these basic debates. For each method, I have summarized the traditional view of its positions in Table 2.2.

A. Ethnography

Ethnography is usually seen as quite well defined in terms of these debates. Methodologically, it is strongly interpretive, attending extensively to multiple subtleties of meaning. It is often narrative, although ethnographies of the interwar and immediate postwar period were often filled with explicit analysis of societies in terms of social functions and formal social structures, such as kinship systems.

Ontologically, too, ethnography has drifted; its earlier incarnations emphasized behavior and social structure more than culture, but the latter has come to dominate it in the last quarter century. Ethnography is almost never conducted in a methodologically individualist vein nor in a strongly realist one. It is also always highly contextualized, although the type of context has differed. Ethnographies of the classical era

Table 2.2

METHODS AND THEIR POSITIONS

Debate	Ethnography	Narration	SCA	Small-N Analysis	Formalization
Debates about Methodology					
Positivism/Interpretivism	interpretivism	interpretivism	positivism	D	positivism
Analysis/Narration	narration?	narration	analysis	D	analysis
Debates about Ontology					
Behaviorism/Culturalism (Social Structure/Culture)	behaviorism → culturalism	~	behaviorism	D	behaviorism
Individualism/Emergentism	emergentism	~	individualism	D	individualism
Realism/Constructionism	constructionism	~	realism	D	realism
Noncontextualism/ Contextualism	contextualism	contextualism	noncontextualism	contextualism	noncontextualism
Debates about Problematics					
Choice/Constraint	~	D	choice?	~	choice
Consensus/Conflict	~	~	~	~	~
Debates about Knowledge					
Transcendent/Situated	situated	situated	transcendent	D	transcendent

Each cell contains the name of one of the positions, if that is what the method involved generally believes. A question mark signifies that a position is not strongly held. D means "denies" the debate is real. A tilde (~) means "indifferent."

tended to isolate societies from larger systems but always treated the local scene in a comprehensively contextual fashion. By contrast, the main focus of contemporary ethnography is precisely the clash of global and local contexts, with much less study of the details of local context. As for problematics, neither choice/constraint nor conflict/consensus has been a strong debate in ethnographic study, although (as in all social sciences) one could see a drift from consensual to conflict positions from 1960 to 1990. Certainly ethnographies have not commonly been done under anything like strong choice assumptions. Finally, ethnography virtually by definition emphasizes situated knowledge. The generation of universal knowledge from ethnography has been very difficult. In the early years, the emphasis on functions and social structures like kinship led to considerable generalizing, but the flood of "cultural analysis" has washed most universalizing out of ethnographic studies. The only universal statements in ethnography today concern the universally creative and interpretive flux of culture and meaning.

B. *Historical Narration*

Like ethnography, historical narration is strongly interpretive. Multiple meanings and ambiguities are its everyday fare. And it is of course narrative, both as a rhetoric and as a mode of questioning and understanding. Narration as a rhetoric has come under attack in the last thirty years, both in the focus on social science history (standard causal analysis as applied to historical problems) and in the newer focus on letting multiple voices speak, which has impugned the grand narratives of nineteenth- and early-twentieth-century historiography. But problems in history are still usually posed narratively—why did A happen and not B?—and social reality is still understood largely as a woven web of stories, not as a systematic social or cultural structure.

Among the ontological debates, historical narration has taken a strong position only on the issue of contextualism, always insisting on the embedding of any historical inquiry in a general knowledge of its time and place. Again, there has been some relaxation, but historical narration remains far more contextualized than nearly any other social scientific method. On the issue of behavior/structure and culture, historical narration has varied, emphasizing now one, now the other. This has been the case with individuals and emergents as well, although the de-emphasis on political history over the last quarter century has generally meant a greater emphasis on emergent groups and their histories. It is the same with realism and constructionism. The inevitably processual character of historical narration inclines it toward a constructionist position, but the mass of detail that must be told in a narrative makes realism an important defense against sheer informational chaos.

In problematics, historical narration has always emphasized a dialogue between choice and constraint. Indeed, one might see this insistent denial of the entire choice/constraint debate as one of the basic marks of historical writing. Both conflict and consensus, on the other hand, have been motivating schemes for historical narration, often being combined in narratives of the exacerbation and reconciliation of conflicts (as in much writing about social movements).

Finally, historical narration, like ethnography, always emphasizes situated knowledge. The last time historians seriously envisioned universal processes was in the mid–nineteenth century—Spenser's social Darwinism and Marx's dialectical materialism are examples—although globalization may be a candidate in the near future. Indeed, world history is enjoying a new vogue, so we may be headed for a new type of universalism in history.

C. Standard Causal Analysis

Standard causal analysis reverses many of the positions of ethnography and narration. It is positivistic, believing that social measurement is possible and indeed necessary, although sometimes difficult in practice. It is unrelentingly analytic, invoking narration only to imagine relations among variables or causal forces.

Ontologically, it has usually emphasized the individual, since it always works with individual units of analysis that are characterized by properties. (One can imagine an emergentist SCA mathematically based on emergent continuities—an SCA based on mathematical topology, for example—but it hasn't "emerged.") SCA has also emphasized behavior/structure more than culture. For the most part, SCA denies context, because contextualism is a major inconvenience to the statistical methods it uses. The whole idea of variables is to remove particular attributes of particular cases from the contexts provided by other attributes of those cases. Realism is likewise a strong assumption of SCA, since it presumes fixed and given meanings.

On problematics, the standard causal position is more open. The sociological version of it is not very welcoming to constraints, since one of the assumptions of its methods is that independent variables are free to determine the dependent variable. In a model of occupational achievement, for example, SCA would not recognize the fact that the overall size of most occupations is determined by forces other than the qualities of the people who go into them. (Occupational size is largely determined by the mode of production in the economy.) There has, however, emerged a small school of sociologist "network analysts" who work under SCA assumptions but study constraint directly. On the conflict/consensus issue, by contrast, standard methods are agnostic. Finally, the standard causal position is overwhelmingly universalist. Indeed, this is one of the foundations of its appeal. Its whole aim is to achieve knowledge transcending locality.

D. Small-N Comparison

As I noted, small-N comparison is a hybrid. It aims to keep the interpretive and narrative subtlety of ethnography and narration but to add to these an analytic strength that echoes standard causal analysis. Ontologically also, small-N comparison has retained the openness of ethnography and narration. It emphasizes neither the individual nor the group, neither behavior/structure nor culture, and has operated on both realist and constructionist assumptions, although like ethnography and narration it leans toward the latter. Like them, too, it is highly contextualized. Indeed, the central point of small-N analysis, when compared with standard causal analysis, is precisely to retain the contextual information that standard causal analysis strips from its multitudes of cases.

By doing this, small-N analysis hopes to produce knowledge that is both situated and universal. On the one hand, the retention of detail in the case studies produces situated, contextualized knowledge; on the other hand, the use of different cases allows the analyst to separate the particular aspects of particular cases from more general processes. As for what it takes to be problematic in social life, small-N analysis has no strong identity, emphasizing neither choice nor constraint, neither conflict nor consensus. By contrast, small-N comparison is uniquely identified by its stand on the aims of knowledge. Its basic aim is to square the methodological circle by combining situated and transcendent knowledge.

E. Formalization

As in many other ways, formalization is the most extreme of the methods discussed here. It is almost absolutely positivistic, although curiously so in that it involves no real measurement. The practice of measurement is unnecessary to it, and indeed in economics, the stronghold of formal analysis, concern with measurement of social facts is probably lower than anywhere else in the social sciences. At the same time, the presumption that accurate and valid measurement is *possible* is an absolute for formalization.

It might seem to go without saying that formalization is analytic rather than narrative, but game theory—which is certainly formalistic—contains at least the beginnings of an abstract approach to narration. Narrative formalization was also characteristic of the literary structuralism of the 1950s, 1960s, and 1970s and entered the social sciences through Lévi-Strauss. But it has not endured as a standard method.

Ontologically, formalization has generally been both individualistic and realist. It has been overwhelmingly concerned with behavior/structure rather than culture and has been acontextual, although formal models of context, like the Schelling segregation models and other contagion models, are not uncommon. But context is, in these models, highly formalized.

As for what it takes to be problematic, formalization has typically attended more to choice than to constraint. It has been agnostic on the conflict/consensus issue but has been absolute in its allegiance to transcendent knowledge.

III. CYCLES OF CRITIQUE

It is thus easy to sketch the basic philosophical stances of the standard methods already introduced. And indeed sketching those stances helps make the methods more clear and comprehensible and emphasizes the ways in which they disagree with one another. Looking at these disagreements, we might conclude that our methods lie on a grand sweep from ethnography and history to small-N analysis, then SCA, then formalization—a grand move from concrete to abstract. Indeed, it is common to run most of the debates discussed in the first part of the chapter into one huge thing, an apparent gradient from interpretive–narrative–emergentist–contextualized–situated knowledge to positive–analytic–individualist–noncontextualized–universal knowledge.

This conflation is a mistake, for a number of reasons. First, there are obvious counterexamples. Ethnography and formalization came together in Lévi-Strauss's attempt to find a formal model for the structure of myths. Well, one might say, that wasn't real formalization. No calculus, no numerical matrices, only a couple of charts and some coding—that's not much formalization. But the deeper point is that Lévi-Strauss did turn toward formalization. He wished to make a syntactic move, in the terms given in Chapter One. That he didn't happen to use the usual machinery of the best-developed formalizations around—microeconomics, game theory, and such—doesn't help us to understand what he was trying to do. What does help us is to see his new method for myth as part of the explanatory program he was trying to create—a syntactic one (with an emphasis on elegant arguments within it), rather than the semantic one that had dominated the study of myth up to that point (which had emphasized the reference between myths and daily life or between myths and social structure).

It was for this reason that I stressed in Chapter One that the three explanatory programs I was discussing were directions rather than specific contents or methods. Abstraction is a magnitude—a distance away from concrete reality. But one can become abstract in several different ways and one can take a new direction any time, anywhere. That is what the idea of explanatory programs emphasizes. It so happens that we have a number of living methodological traditions, and they happen to have embodied explanatory programs in various ways, just as they have taken various stances on the great debates just listed. But they are living and changing traditions, and it is possible for them to turn in pretty much any explanatory direction any time they like.

The conflating of all the different debates into one big opposition or gradient is wrong for another reason, too. A short reflection on our methods shows that far from lying on a gradient, they are in fact organized more in a circle. We are all familiar with cyclic order from the children's game Rock-Paper-Scissors; our methods set up a methodological

Rock-Paper-Scissors game. Put any two studies using slightly different methods together, and one will seem to have a more effective method. We will then find that this method can be improved further by moving toward yet a third method. And that third method may in turn be improved by moving toward the first!

For example, suppose we want to pursue Lévi-Strauss's topic of myth. We do an ethnography, gathering all the myths of the Bella Coola, a people of western Canada. Reflection on our notes makes us see a close connection between the mythic structure and the clan structure, so we decide the myth system is in fact a loose cultural picture of the clans. The clans use the myth system to talk about, modify, undercut, and otherwise manipulate the strong social structure that is the everyday reality of clan life. Naturally, we would want to discuss this data with other students of myth, comparing our theories with theirs.

Systematic data on the Bella Coola, like data on hundreds of other societies, has been collected in something called the Human Relations Area Files. Using this enormous database, someone might develop a classification and coding scheme for the myth systems of *dozens* of primitive societies, as well as for other aspects of cultural and social structure. With those codes, he or she could then do an excellent SCA, showing that type of myth system could be predicted by knowing, say, the type of lineage system (patrilineal, matrilineal, bilateral), certain aspects of the gender division of labor, and type of contact with the Western world. This knowledge would reduce our Bella Coola study to one example of a phenomenon we now "understand" because of the "more general analysis."

One could imagine a series of such SCA studies of myth and other aspects of primitive societies, a literature developing its own internal debates and questions by changing the variables observed, the types of analysis, and so on. But one can also imagine a historian studying the process through which cultural artifacts and myths were collected in a number of tribes. It might well turn out that the myths and physical artifacts were produced for, and therefore determined by, the demands of anthropologists, museum workers, and other collectors of "primitive material." As is true of many of the Northwest totem poles, these myths may have been produced "for the anthropology trade" as much as for the primitive societies themselves (see Cole 1985). In fact, the social structures of these tribes may have been reconstructed in various ways by contact with modern societies; we now know, for example, that the famous potlatch ceremony of the Bella Coola and the Kwakiutl as it was studied by the early anthropological collectors was in large part a *creation* of that contact (Cole 1985; Cole and Chaikin 1990). On such an argument, the SCA tradition goes up in smoke. It is talking about a causal situation that wasn't in any sense real. So we give up on our SCA tradition just as we gave up on the ethnographic tradition, and we begin a literature of historical inquiry into the nature of contact between primitive societies and the West. (Indeed, such a literature has emerged, although not out of critique of an SCA literature but rather out of critique of ethnography per se.)

We can, however, imagine an ethnographer going to the field deliberately to study culture contact. And we can imagine that ethnographer telling some historians of contact with the West that they have missed the extraordinary creativity with which primitive societies reshape the cultural and social materials that come to them through contact. So here we are back at ethnography again, right where we started before our little detour through SCA and historical analysis. Moreover, perhaps that ethnographer has just read some game theory (which is, after all, a type of formalization) and thinks that we should perhaps recast the process of culture contact as a repeated-play Chicken game, in which every time contact recurs, both sides attempt to enforce their interpretations of the situation until at the last moment one or the other transforms its interpretation through a complete redefinition. But this redefinition lasts only until the next play, and so on.

This is exactly a Rock-Paper-Scissors situation. SCA trumps ethnography by generalizing. History trumps SCA by historicizing its categories. Ethnography trumps history by undercutting the very idea of historical continuity, invoking formalization into the bargain. Note that each of these trumpings involves a move to a new dimension of difference between methods, and thus each methodological replacement is really an assertion that the dimension emphasized by the *replacing* method is more important than the one *replaced*. SCA trumps ethnography by asserting that generalization is more important than detail. History trumps SCA by asserting that historical verisimilitude is more important than simple generality. Ethnography trumps history by asserting that the power of cultural reinterpretation can undercut our belief in any historical continuities.

It seems likely, then, that each method can trump all the others, although in different ways. There are thus many different methodological "cycles" like the one above. Moreover, nearly all of these trumpings have been tried and have led each methodological community to forms of revisionism that try to deal with the shortcomings other communities have pointed out. These, too, complicate the methodological landscape.

Even worse, each method offers a metacritique of the others. That is, each method can be used to analyze the *practitioners* of the others; one can do an ethnography of historians or an SCA of formalists, for example.

It is useful to run through all of these critiques and trumpings and revisions, just to put them all down in one place. In part, I do this so that the reader will not take them too seriously. When we see them all together, it is hard to believe that these little round-robins amount to much. But I also provide this list to emphasize again that *there is no inherent gradient or order to methods*. Each method privileges some aspects of analysis over others, and as a consequence each is more or less important as we attend to this or that criterion for our analyses. I have gathered all of these comments in Table 2.3, showing both the metacritiques and the directed critiques. I also show examples of responses (implicit or explicit) to the directed critiques.

A. *Ethnography*

Ethnography argues that historical narration overlooks the extraordinary variety of human life in its attempt to find the trends and general principles of an age. Responding to this critique, historians throughout the 1960s, 1970s, and 1980s moved toward history "from the bottom up," studying the "people without history," often employing an oral history that looks no different from ethnography. Although all of these studies were in part inspired by a political impulse to study the

Table 2.3

METACRITIQUES, CRITIQUES, AND RESPONSES

Method	Metacritique	Critique	Response
Ethnography	Others lack ethnography of selves.		
Historical Narration		misses extraordinary variety of the social world	history from the ground up; oral history
Small-N Comparison		compares sites despite major differences; doesn't necessarily have same researchers at all sites	
SCA		uses worthless or meaningless data; assigns meanings arbitrarily	focus groups
Formalization			
Historical Narration	Others lack sense of their own history.		
Ethnography		is static; misses change of meaning; lacks history of its own terms, of its types of analysis, of itself	rise of work combining history and ethnography—for example, Sidney Mintz, Eric Wolf
Small-N Comparison		lacks primary data; misses context	primary-data-based comparative historical sociology
SCA		ignores contingency; lacks account of action; cannot represent "history" of its variables	social science history; conditional models; periodized time series analysis
Formalization		assumes that underlying model does not change	evolutionary algorithms

SCA	Others' methodological allegiances can be explained by various causal forces. (implicit only)		
Ethnography		lacks generalization; lacks causal analysis; is unfalsifiable; uses unreliable measurement; is not scientific	group ethnographies combining multiple sites
Historical Narration		lacks generalization; lacks causal analysis; is unfalsifiable	comparative historical sociology
Small-N Comparison		uses case numbers too small for generalizing; retains meaningless detail, keeps worst of both worlds	qualitative comparative analysis (QCA)—Charles Ragin
Formalization		lacks content; accepts bad data	

Formalization		
Ethnography	lacks theory	Claude Lévi-Strauss on mythological analysis; Harrison White on kinship
Historical Narration	lacks theory	rational choice history—Hilton Root, Margaret Weir
Small-N Comparison	lacks theory	
SCA	lacks theory	testing of game theoretic hypotheses

The table is not saturated in the sense that every possible cell is filled in. I have left blanks where I am not aware of a major critical literature or response. In addition, the "responses" here do not necessarily come from the criticized community. Comparative historical sociology came from sociology, not history, although it responds to the SCA critique of "uncausal" historical work.

forgotten and downtrodden, they were also rooted both directly and indirectly in an ethnographic impulse to get closer to the data underneath the "grand syntheses" that ignored so much.

Ethnography argues that in small-N analysis there are fundamental problems of comparability between cases, even if the analysis involved is itself ethnographic. Small-N analysis contextualizes, but not enough. Against SCA, the ethnographic case is much clearer. Ethnography thinks that social facts derive their meaning from other facts around them. To treat social facts as "variables" on universal scales (where a given fact has a given meaning irrespective of the other facts in its context) destroys that meaning. Ethnography therefore regards coding and quantification with profound suspicion and believes that the data on which SCA bases itself are quite literally meaningless. While there has not been a direct infusion of ethnography into SCA because of this critique, there *has* been an enormous increase in the use of focus groups and other quasi-ethnographic devices to make sure that questionnaires make sense with respect to the people being surveyed, rather than simply coming from the minds of surveyors, as they often did in the early days.

Oddly enough, ethnography and formalization have had a long-standing flirtation. They share a certain love of complexity. For ethnography, this is a complexity of facts and events. For formalization, it is a complexity of formal details and inferences, very much evident in the dozens of different games (Chicken, Tit for Tat, Prisoners' Dilemma, and so on) invented by the game theorists. Lévi-Straussian anthropology was highly formal, as was cognitive anthropology in the 1960s and as is much of anthropological linguistics today. For their part, the formalists had a fine time trying to mathematize the kinship systems of the world. This odd flirtation between what are apparently the ends of a concrete-abstract scale underscores the cyclic nature of methods. The ethnographic discipline of anthropology has been far more hospitable to formalization than to any version of SCA.

The ethnographic metacritique of other methods is carried out in the now widespread ethnographic analysis of groups of natural and social scientists. The content of the critique is simple enough. Without a serious ethnographic analysis of their practices and beliefs, social scientists cannot understand what they themselves are doing. Their surface discourse—of methods and theories and findings—in fact covers a much more complex set of cultural structures. What is going on may then not be "social science" but rather making sense of local anomalies in the data, controlling the way in which surveys simplify reality for large or small political reasons, and so on. In this way, ethnography can claim that methodological discussion is in practice a cover for other agendas: personal, institutional, societal, political.

B. Historical Narration

The historians have a different metacritique. For them, the great problem of social science is that it does not historicize itself. That is, methodological communities lack a sense of their history and hence a sense of the transitory nature of the very terminologies with which they debate central methodological and theoretical issues. Until social scientists understand themselves as working in cultural communities that interact in highly structured and even ritualized ways, they will be forced by their own rhetorics and symbols to walk on a treadmill, imagining that they are advancing, but in fact going nowhere. Indeed, it may well not be *possible* to go in any direction. We may simply be wandering around aimlessly. Historical analysis emphasizes the role of contingency and accident in all methodological development.

If we turn to the specific critiques that historical analysis levels at other methods, we find an interesting variety. Historical analysis criticizes ethnography for being static. By going to a single place at a single time, an ethnographer loses the ability to distinguish things that are changing from things that are not. Everything that endures as long as the ethnographic encounter looks permanent. Indeed, from 1970 onward, writers have criticized the classic ethnographies of the interwar period for treating the fleeting moments of the last stages of colonialism as if they were stable moments of "traditional societies."

Against small-N analysis—usually, comparative historical work—history's claim has been quite simple. Small-N analysts typically do not use large amounts of primary documents and typically know far less than do specialists on one case. Historians think small-N analysts simply don't know their cases. By contrast, the historical case against SCA is much more vague. In fact, there has been a substantial move to marry SCA methods to historical questions, in the large and amorphous movement called social science history. (Not all of the participants in this have been historians; there have been many historical demographers, economists, and sociologists involved as well.) The deeper "historical" case against SCA is that reality happens not in isolated events and properties, as the SCA practice of variables analysis assumes, but rather in cascades of action and reaction, choice and constraint. SCA really has no account of action and reaction whatsoever; its only standard method for analyzing action is to estimate the effects of different variables on the waiting time till some dependent event occurs—that's hardly history. Finally, historical narration argues that SCA's variables have histories, which are always ignored. One cannot really do over-time models of changes in the relationship between occupation and education because the very categories— the names and contents of occupations and the names and contents of types of education—change over any time period worth analyzing.

Against formalization, the chief argument of historical analysis is that it always presupposes a formal model that doesn't change, whether that model is game theoretic or microeconomic or structuralist. But it is the cardinal presupposition of historical analysis that anything, even the very rules of the game, can change. To the extent that there are universal rules, they are contentless, definitional truisms—"people do what they want to do" and that sort of thing. Interestingly, there have been occasional outbreaks of formalist history, generally coming from outside history as a discipline. Nicolas Rashevsky once wrote an amusing book called *Looking at History through Mathematics*, and more recently there have been various rational-choice models applied to historical events. But no one has ever seriously attempted the central task of making formal models themselves fully historical (by making the rules of the games completely internal, a part of the game). This question belongs to the computer science field of recursive theory and will no doubt be addressed soon enough.

C. Standard Causal Analysis

SCA's critiques of other forms of method are familiar. SCA condemns ethnography for not allowing general conclusions, for being unfalsifiable, for using unreliable and unreplicable subjective "measurement"—in short, for not being scientific. SCA condemns historical analysis for many of the same reasons, although particularly emphasizing the fact that historical analysis is not "causal analysis." By this criticism, SCA means two things, one more limited than the other. The limited critique is that historical analysis doesn't produce coefficients telling us how much of each independent factor is involved in the dependent result. Historical narration is more likely to combine the factors in a story, to envision multiple contingencies and interdependencies. This limited critique is largely definitional; SCA is saying that history isn't SCA, which does produce such coefficients and, more important, claims that story telling is not a legitimate form of explanation.

The broader critique is more profound. SCA legitimately argues that historical analysis rarely if ever investigates *common* forms of "stories" across cases; it never attempts even "historical," much less causal, generalization. This critique gave rise to comparative historical sociology, a form of small-N analysis designed to deliberately evaluate different causal patterns in small numbers of cases. It also led to various forms of narrative positivism, which attempt to directly measure and analyze large numbers of historical "story" patterns like careers or revolutions. SCA then criticized these revisions themselves. It criticized small-N analysis (in the guise of comparative historical sociology) for *still* having too few cases for effective generalization, while it criticized narrative positivism for not having enough causal analysis.[2]

Against formalization, SCA argues that it is too vague and contentless. There is no necessary connection between a formal model and any particular set of data, as we have seen before. This is both a theoretical and a practical objection. On the one hand is the theoretical problem that any given social situation can be represented by dozens of formal models with varying assumptions and implications. On the other is the practical problem that formalists have often been extremely cavalier about data.

As a metacritique, SCA is less direct than are ethnography and history, whose metacritiques are almost ad hominem. They can point to particular misunderstandings, particular anachronisms. They can be and are used as weapons in intellectual debate. The SCA metacritique is more implicit. It implies that one could model the output of the various disciplines and show that various causal factors—the talent of practitioners, the levels of funding, the structure of interlocking elites—might explain that output. It is interesting that hardly anyone today bothers to do such models either as critique or even as simple sociology of science, although there is certainly a persistent folk belief among SCA practitioners that the form and content of ethnography, narration, and small-N analysis are determined by the (supposed) lack of mathematical skill among those who use them.

D. Formalization

The formalists, too, spend little of their time in metacritique. They don't bother to write models for others' scholarship, although I suppose they could easily enough. Rather, they have a single common critique that they apply to nearly all other forms of method. That critique is simply that all other methods use causal and explanatory arguments whose implications have not been well worked out. So the first few pages of an SCA analysis of why people stay at jobs might contain two or three "hypotheses," which would basically be stories about plausible behaviors of certain kinds of workers under certain kinds of conditions. An economist could easily write twenty pages of calculus to justify (or reject) just one of those stories. The same applies—only more so—for ethnography, historical analysis, and small-N arguments. For the formalist, these methods are simply not thought out. Not only are the arguments in each study undeveloped in formal terms, but there is also no broader, purely theoretical argument that holds them in a firm common framework. As far as formalists are concerned, this is just as true of SCA, with its somewhat ad hoc, just-so "theorizing," as it is of ethnography and historical analysis, with their attempts to explain particular cases. All the same, there are formalist connections to nearly all of the other methods, sometimes originating on the formalist side, sometimes on the other.

E. Small-N Analysis

Small-N analysis is in many ways a compromise method designed to deal with all of these criticisms. Small-N ethnography tries to avoid the no-generalization critique SCA makes of ethnography, just as small-N historical analysis tries to avoid the no-causal-analysis critique SCA makes of historical analysis. At the same time, small-N comparison tries to avoid the meaningless-variables and no-events critiques that go the other way. Like most compromise strategies, small-N analysis often ends up falling between two stools. As is also implicit in the idea of compromise, small-N analysis does not have any general metacritique of the other methods.

IT IS THUS CLEAR that each method considered here has solid and profound objections to all the others. The result, as I noted at the outset, is that methods have a cyclical relationship. Each one is capable of correcting the others. Indeed, as we have seen in this discussion, many of these corrections have taken form in substantial bodies of literature. But when all of these various corrections are laid out together, we find ourselves in a labyrinth where any method can be found both superior *and* inferior to any other.

IV. FROM CRITIQUE TO HEURISTIC

It is useful to summarize the argument of the chapter so far. In the first section, I discussed some basic debates in the social sciences. In the second, I pointed out how the methods of the preceding chapter are defined in terms of these basic debates. At this point, it was noted, a standard methodology text would launch into the details of each basic method, leaving the profound differences of assumptions as simply something to take notice of and then move past. There would be a single chapter on each method, elaborating the positions inherent in these debates and showing how the methods go about proposing questions, designing studies, acquiring data, and drawing inferences.

Instead, I showed that the usual way of relating these methods to one another is wrong. The apparent gradient from one methodological type to another is indeed merely apparent; methodological critiques actually go around in circles. With all of these critiques laid out in one place, one can see that as a system they do not form a logical structure. (As a result, most writing that attempts self-conscious methodological critique is nonsense or pure polemic.)

The more important reason for setting out these arguments in one place is to begin to show how, in the hands of some scholars, problems and critiques become creative. It is by making these critiques that we have in many cases figured out new things to say in our research. Not that the new things are necessarily better in any global sense. They may be better locally, but overall the cyclical character of methodological critique guarantees, as I have noted, that there is no real "better" in a global sense. What *is* better in the global sense is to know more or to know reality in more detailed ways or in more different and mutually challenging ways—or something like that. It is as if we were interested not in separating the true from the false but simply in trying to say all of the things we could possibly say about social life, given an ideal that we somehow be rigorous in our ways of saying them. (Put another way, we have to define truth in a much more flexible way if we are going to understand what we do as social scientists.)

So mutual methodological critique is important not because it makes us more right but because it gives us more—and particularly more complicated—things to say. That is, mutual methodological critique is useful heuristically. It generates new ideas. Seeing SCA from the viewpoint of ethnography leads SCA to produce more interesting and more complex results. Seeing historical narration from the viewpoint of formalization produces surprising insights. Sometimes such critiques lead to whole new methodological communities, hybridizing older methods. Social science history emerged out of the SCA critique of historical narration, while history "from the bottom up" emerged out of an ethnographic critique of historical narration. Both were exciting and intellectually decisive movements.

We have, then, already seen our first heuristic move. It is the move you make when you ask yourself how someone from another methodological approach sees what you are doing. Mutual methodological critique is thus the first of the general heuristics I discuss. The next three chapters discuss other kinds of heuristics. In Chapter Three, I discuss the idea of heuristic generally, examining what we mean by a trick or rule for coming up with new ideas. I also discuss the two simplest means for producing such ideas. The first is the additive heuristic of normal science, making a new idea by making a minor change in an old idea and repeating the analysis. The second is the heuristic of topics, using lists of standard ideas to avoid getting stuck in one way of thinking.

In Chapters Four and Five, I turn from such global heuristic strategies to more particular rules for producing new ideas. Some of these are ways of searching elsewhere for ideas; others are content-free rules for changing arguments. Some are ways of changing the description of the events we are trying to theorize about; some are ways of changing the way we tell stories about those events. All are potential tools for transforming existing arguments into new ones.

Chapter Six returns to the heuristics implicit in the mutual methodological critiques just discussed. The heuristic fertility of mutual methodological critique can be extended by a further analysis of the basic debates with which I began this chapter. Much of the power of mutual critique comes from a peculiar quality of those debates. It turns out that they are fractals. That is, they are not simple linear scales from positivism to interpretation, say, or from narration to analysis. Rather, they are continuously subdividing structures. The positivists fight with the interpretivists, but then each group divides within itself into positivists and interpretivists, and so on and on.

To take an example, positivist sociologists like to do surveys, and interpretivist sociologists like to do ethnography. But among those who do surveys, some are very worried about exactly how respondents understand a question, while others trust random error to take care of interpretive problems. Once again, we have interpretivists and positivists—only *within* what we thought was a group of positivists. This happens on the interpretive side as well. There we will have, on the one hand, the indexer-coder types, who carefully index their field notes and develop "hypotheses" based on the patterns of codes they see, and, on the other hand, the deep interpretivists, who want to consider the way particular words were used in particular sentences. Oddly enough the random-error surveyors (positivist positivists) in some ways have more in common with the indexer-coder ethnographers (positivist interpretivists) than with the respondent-bias surveyors (interpretivist positivists)—not in all ways, but in some.

I could multiply examples, but the point is made. These basic debates are *not* grand, fixed positions taken once and for all in one's choice of method. They arise as choices day in, day out. They pervade the process of research. And hardly anyone makes them the same way in all contexts and at all moments. Chapter Six shows how this complex and fractal character of the basic debates makes them into a crucial heuristic resource for social science. Just as the trumping critiques of the last section provide bases for whole new literatures, so too do the fractal debates at the heart of social science provide endless ways to come up with new ideas and even new ways to imagine our questions. That is exactly what we mean by heuristic.

Chapter Three
INTRODUCTION TO HEURISTICS

I. THE IDEA OF HEURISTIC

The classic story about heuristics tells how Archimedes jumped out of the bathtub and ran naked through the streets of Syracuse, shouting "I've found it." As he had watched water slosh out of the tub, he had suddenly realized that something that weighed the same as his body but was more dense would make less water slosh out of the tub. Hence, if the supposedly golden crown of his friend King Heiron was actually made of a cheaper silver alloy, it would displace more water than an all-gold crown, because silver is less dense than gold. So he could tell whether the crown was made entirely of gold without melting it.

What Archimedes actually shouted, of course, was not "I've found it," but "Eureka," the first-person singular perfect of the Greek verb *heuriskein*, meaning "to find."[1] From this word comes the English word *heuristic*, which denotes the study of how to find things out—the discipline, as it were, of discovery. The Archimedes story is a good place to start thinking about heuristic. Archimedes had a problem. Bobbing in the bathtub gave him the solution. And so heuristic is the science of finding new ways to solve problems, the science, as it were, of bathtubs. Thus, in computer science, *heuristic programming* refers to programming that takes an experimental approach to problem solution rather than an analytically exact one.[2]

Most modern writing about heuristic comes from mathematics. Mathematicians often have particular problems to solve: how to solve the normal distribution integral (hint: you can't do it analytically), how to create a perfect pentagon, how to categorize all the possible types of disconnection in six-space, and so on. Mathematicians often know or suspect the answer they seek but need to be sure of how one gets there. Even when they don't know the answer, they usually have a clear idea of what an answer looks like. In such a context, heuristic means thinking creatively about how to get from problem to solution. Often one builds out from the problem on the one hand and from the solution on the other until the two halves meet in the middle like a bridge built from two banks.

The greatest modern writer on heuristic, the probabilist George Pólya, wrote his brilliant *How to Solve It* precisely about such mathematical problems. Pólya presented a large number of tricks and schemes for making difficult problems solvable. He thought there were four crucial steps to problem solution: understanding the problem, developing a plan to solve it, carrying that plan out, and looking back from the solution. Each of these steps involved a number of questions and tasks:

1. **Understand the Problem:**

   What is the unknown? What are the data? What are the "conditions"?

   Draw a figure. Introduce suitable notation.

   Separate the parts of the conditions.

2. **Devise a Plan:**

   Have you seen this problem before or something like it?

   Do you know another problem with the same unknown?

   If you have a related problem and its solution, how can you use that here?

   Can you restate the problem? Solve a part of it? Solve an analogous problem? Solve a bigger problem of which it is a part?

3. **Carry Out the Plan:**

   Check each step. Are they really correct? Can you prove it?

4. **Look Back:**

   Can you check the result? Can you derive the result differently?

   Can you use the result to solve another problem?

   (1957:xvi–xvii)

Most of Pólya's book is a "dictionary of heuristic"—really a set of meditations on various topics relevant to discovery. Some of these topics are strategies for problem solving: auxiliary problems, decomposing and recombining, mathematical induction, variation of the problem, working backward. Others are extended essays on the questions listed under items 1–4 above.

But in the social sciences we often have a different situation. We often don't see ahead of time exactly what the problem is, much less do we have an idea of the solution. We often come at an issue with only a gut feeling that there is something interesting about it. We often don't know even what an answer ought to look like. Indeed, figuring out what the puzzle really is and what the answer ought to look like often happen in parallel with finding the answer itself. This is why many if not most writers of social science dissertations and books write the introductions to their dissertations and books *last*, after all the substantive chapters have been written. Their original research proposals usually turn out to have just been hunting licenses, most often licenses to hunt animals very different from the ones that have ended up in the undergraduate thesis or the doctoral dissertation.

This difference between mathematics and the social sciences means that I do *not* necessarily assume here that the reader is someone at the beginning of a research project, looking for new ideas. Most teaching on methods assumes that the student will start a research project with a general question, then narrow that to a focused question, which will dictate the kind of data needed, which will in turn support an analysis designed to answer the focused question. Nothing could be further from reality. Most research projects—from first-year undergraduate papers to midcareer multiyear, multi-investigator projects—start out as general interests in an area tied up with hazy notions about some possible data, a preference for this or that kind of method, and as often as not a preference for certain kinds of results. Most research projects advance on all of these fronts at once, the data getting better as the question gets more focused, the methods more firmly decided, and the results more precise. At some point—the dissertation-proposal hearing for graduate students, the grant-proposal stage for faculty, the office hour with the supervising faculty member for any serious undergraduate paper—an attempt is made to develop a soup-to-nuts account of the research in the traditional order. Now emerges the familiar format of puzzle leading to literature review leading to formal question, data, and methods. Even then, the soup-to-nuts menu is likely to be for a different meal than the one that ends up in the final paper.

As any senior researcher can tell you, the typical grant-funded project has some of its final results in hand by this mid-point in the research process. Put another way, you can't tell a granting agency what you are going to do until you've very nearly finished doing it. And indeed, many faculty use grant funds from one project to do their *next* project, which they apply for—when *it* is nearly done—to get funds to do the project after that. (That is, expecting you to know exactly what you are going to do ahead of time is completely unrealistic in the social sciences.) So the first version of a traditional proposal is pretty tentative. The real reason for forcing research into that format is that the format makes it easier to see what remains to be done and what hasn't worked so far.

All of which means that I am *not* assuming that the reader is reading this book in hopes of getting an idea, which will then lead to focused questions, and data, and so on. The gambits I discuss can be useful at any time in a project, because data, methods, and theory will all be recast again and again throughout the course of any research project.

This talk about senior researchers may seem to suggest that my argument is losing its original focus on the beginning student. So a word is useful here about the stages of an intellectual life. It turns out that heuristics do different things for us at different ages.

I noted in my remarks To the Reader that a common problem among students is a feeling that one has nothing to say. And the principal theme of this book is resolving that problem by finding bases for new ideas. The problem of having nothing (new) to say is for the most part a problem that arises because you, the student, are doing social science for the first time. So you find the huge variety of things that *could* be said almost as overwhelming as the huge diversity of things that *have been* said.

In this common situation, heuristic helps you deal with both problems. On the one hand, it gives you tools to question what has been said, transforming it into new ideas and new views. On the other hand, steady practice of heuristic will teach you rules for separating good things that could be said from bad ones, as we shall see in Chapter Seven.

Having a hard time deciding what to say is to some extent a problem of people who don't have a ready-made stance toward social life. We all know many people who *do* have such a ready-made stance, for that is the position of people who have a strong political interest of some kind. Whatever the issue raised, people with such political interests have a stance on it, a way of thinking about it. Often they even have stock questions and puzzles about it (as in the feminist's questions "what about *women* and social networks?" "what about a *gendered* concept of narrative?" and so on). These flow from their relatively one-sided view of social life, which is somewhat easier and in some ways less intellectually self-defeating than a position that tries to see a problem from all sides. The proverbial view from nowhere is willy-nilly characteristic of people just starting out in social science or of people who don't yet have particular commitments, and it is much harder to work with than the more comfortable view from a point.

This comfortable one-sidedness, which only strongly political people have from the start, is a quality we all achieve after our early outings as social scientists. It is a kind of second stage of our development. You don't necessarily become dominated by this or that political concern, but you decide you're a Marxist or a Weberian or Foucauldian, and voilà—for any given problem you have a viewpoint and even some standard questions. At that point, you need heuristics not so much to get started as to free yourself from the restrictions of your point of view. Otherwise, you are always writing papers in the form of "a neo-institutionalist view of church organization" or "Bourdieu's habitus as an educational concept" or "Marxian theories of education" and wondering why no one outside your camp gets excited.

The reason you want to free yourself from those restrictions is of course that there are always lots of other people around who aren't Marxists or Weberians or whatever you are. Those people always seem to have their own well-worked-out views of issues and problems and data. If you can't learn to think in their modalities, you can't talk to them. So now you begin to use heuristics not just to loosen up your own views. You try to master the basic viewpoints and even the heuristic repertoires of *other* stances toward the social world. This is the third stage of a social scientist's intellectual development. We look for this in good students when we say, "OK, now what's the game-theory approach to that question?" and then follow with "Would a Weberian be comfortable with that?"

You have come of age as a social scientist when you know all of the diverse second-level repertoires of concepts and questions so well that you use heuristic strategies to set various points of view against one another. This is the fourth and final level of social science work. You start using the different standard stances to question one another; each becomes the others' heuristic. This is to some extent what I meant by the discussions of mutual criticism between methods in the preceding chapter. Each stance begins to challenge all the others.

More important, you can do something at this advanced stage that many never manage. You can combine stances into far more complex forms of questioning than any one of them can produce alone. An example from the arts will show what I mean. In the early 1780s, Mozart found some Bach manuscripts and was amazed by them. He decided to learn to write Baroque-style music, and his C Minor Mass shows that he could indeed write such music as easily as he could write the classical style for which he is more famous. So in the opera *Don Giovanni*, he defined different characters by writing music for them in different styles. The arias for Donna Elvira—the most traditional of the five women Don Giovanni hustles in the opera—are written in a rigid Baroque style that would have struck any listener at the time as completely old-fashioned, just right for the old-fashioned woman Donna Elvira is meant to be. Don Giovanni's music is much more current, befitting his energetic but sleazy self, while the music of his servant-fix-it man, the scamp Leporello, is written in the rhythms of the peasant dances of the time. For Mozart, different styles are not a problem but a resource (see Allenbrook 1983). Only a master of many styles can make them talk to each other in this way. At the highest level of social science, this is what serious heuristic can accomplish.

In short, heuristic is useful to all of us, each at our own levels in the social sciences. But while the basic repertoire of heuristics can be deployed in a number of ways and at a number of levels, it is still a unified repertoire. I begin, then, by discussing in the rest of this chapter the two simplest means for producing new ideas: the additive heuristic that we call normal science and the use of heuristic "topics," or commonplaces.

II. THE ROUTINE HEURISTICS OF NORMAL SCIENCE

George Pólya argued that "[t]he aim of heuristic is to study the methods and rules of discovery and invention" (1957:112). That might make us think that discovery can be made utterly routine; we learn some rules, turn a crank, and voilà—discoveries! But Pòlya clearly meant something more as well. Heuristic *does* go beyond the routine ways we have for producing discoveries. Yet before seeking those, we need to think for a moment about the routine roads.

Thomas Kuhn has provided what for many people is the standard account of discovery, both routine and nonroutine. When Kuhn wrote *The Structure of Scientific Revolutions*, he aimed to replace what we might call the big-edifice model of science. On this model, science at any given time is a big structure of accepted facts, theories, and methods. Scientists are perpetually making new conjectures, testing them on reality with various methods, and then finding them rejected or accepted. If accepted, they become part of the edifice; if not, they don't. The model is gradualist and incremental. Science grows bit by bit, like a big brick building being put up on a firm foundation. We might occasionally replace sizable walls, but we spend most of our time tuck-pointing or building small additions.

To Kuhn as to many others, this vision of science seemed inaccurate. Most major scientific theories seemed to burst on the world like the revolutions of Copernicus, Newton, Darwin, and so on. They were hardly gradualist. Kuhn resolved this dilemma by separating normal science from paradigm-changing science. He argued that science is organized in paradigms, within which research happens incrementally. Little results pile up. New parts of the building are built. Decayed bricks are replaced. But as this normal science goes on, some stubborn realities refuse to fit. These anomalies pile up to the side. They are attributed to mistaken observation, errors in analysis, and so on. Once the pile of anomalies becomes very large, someone sees that by looking at everything differently—different method, different theory, different interpretation of findings— one can account for everything the old paradigm covered as well as for all the anomalies. Kuhn called this transformation a paradigm shift. It embraces new methods, new theories, even new definitions of the facts of the real world. It means tearing the old building down and building a new one with the leftovers, the anomalies, and some new materials.

As this description implies, the central heuristic rule of normal science—science *within* paradigms—is simple addition. If one is an ethnographer, one studies a new tribe or a new situation. If one is a historian, one chronicles a new nation or a new profession or a new war. If one is an SCA analyst, one uses a new independent variable or sometimes even a new dependent variable; one gets a new data set with which to study an old problem or asks an old question in a new way; one tries a new model. If one is a formalist, one changes the rules a bit and re-computes the equilibriums or the parameters of the consequent structure or whatever. If one is a small-N analyst, one adds a few more cases or goes into more detail with the cases one has or perhaps adds a new dimension of analysis.

There are several versions of this more-of-the-same heuristic. The simplest is more data: we take the same ideas to a new place. To be sure, the ethnographer with a new case and the SCA scholar with a new data set are usually not just adding another example. Usually there are minor differences that enable the new data to improve old ideas rather than simply repeat them. But for the beginning social scientist, the normal-science heuristic of "it works here, but will it work there?" is a perfectly fine opening for a research project.

The second version of addition is the addition of some new dimension of analysis. Usually this is a minor dimension. Major recastings are the objects of the stronger heuristics I discuss below. But under this heading we have, for example, the huge number of SCA studies of the form "I know that x leads to y; suppose now I introduce controls for s, t, and u." For example, women are less likely to end up in the natural sciences and mathematics. Will this be true if we control for native ability? for college major? for parental encouragement? for choice of high school classes? and so on. Or consider the long-standing historical finding that the revolutionary political parties of the nineteenth century usually had their origins among artisans rather than among unskilled town laborers or agricultural laborers. Was this also true in areas where artisans were few? Was it true in Catholic as well as Protestant regions? east of the Elbe? and so on.

Finally, addition sometimes takes the form of adding a new model or methodological wrinkle or theoretical twist. For an ethnographer of science, this might be taking a more careful look at the exact language that was used in interviews, to see whether the order in which scientists said certain things revealed new aspects of their assumptions. For a rational-choice modeler, this might be trying four or five different forms of "game," rather than just one or two, to understand a particular bargaining structure. For an SCA analyst, it might be putting exponential terms into the equation, to see whether certain independent variables had not only linear but also nonlinear effects.

All of these—from simply adding data to adding a new dimension for analysis to adding a new methodological or theoretical wrinkle—are basically minor, incremental additions. They are the tuck-pointing and reshingling and addition-building of normal science. They are the conservative strategy for social scientists, and it should come as no surprise that graduate students—the most conservative of all social scientists (because they have the most at risk)—should be assiduous practitioners of the additive heuristic. Libraries are filled with unpublished doctoral dissertations that carry out such additive projects. Scholarly journals receive dozens of submissions based on them.

Such studies are profoundly useful. One brilliant contribution does not fully establish a new argument. Adding new cases or variables or rules is always a useful first step in the full evaluation of ideas. And so it is right and fitting that most of us begin our careers with the additive heuristic, and it is not at all surprising that many of us never leave it.

But the ultimate aim of heuristic is to improve on such normal science. Remember Pólya's definition: "The aim of heuristics is to study the methods and rules of discovery and invention." Invention is what we seek, not just addition. How exactly does one go about creating rules for invention?

III. TOPICS AND COMMONPLACES

There is, it turns out, something of a tradition about invention. It is not found in the sciences but rather in the field of rhetoric. We often use "rhetoric" as a negative word, to label tricks of language or argument. We think of rhetoric as false or at least deceptive. But the ancient writers on rhetoric—people like Isocrates, Aristotle, Cicero, and Quintilian—were mainly concerned with training people as knowledgeable speakers in public settings or as articulate experts in legal settings. And so for them, rhetoric was a good thing, both positive and creative.

The ability to come up with dozens of arguments was central to the classical writers' vision of rhetoric. (Ideally one could do this on one's feet, talking, but in practice speeches were written ahead of time and rehearsed extensively.) Rhetoric textbooks customarily began with a section entitled *inventio*. (*Inventio* is the Latin word; the Greek for this was *heuresis*, from the same root as *heuristic*. See Clarke 1953:7.) This section covered the many ways to think up or invent arguments. The most general ways to do so were called topics and included extremely abstract things like "sameness," "difference," and "genus and species." More concrete sources for arguments were called commonplaces, which were familiar notions, like the idea that criminals did or did not keep committing the same crime— common beliefs that often came in pairs, one on each side of an argument.

Apprentice speakers learned huge lists of topics and commonplaces and their subdivisions. Mastery of such lists was considered the foundation for effective argument. It is hardly surprising that in time there were complaints that oratory had become boring. What had been meant as a guide to inventing new ideas had become a machine producing endlessly familiar ones.

We social scientists have such rhetorical forms, topics, and commonplaces ourselves. The most famous—as familiar to high school students in America as the six parts of a classical speech were to similar students two millennia ago—is "compare and contrast." (It was on Aristotle's and Cicero's lists, too.) "Pros and cons" is another enduring rhetorical form, also on most ancient lists, as it is in the repertoire of most scholars today. Each of these rhetorical forms can be invoked in the heat of argument to provide a prefabricated layout for a discussion. And each can sometimes become very mechanical.

But the use of rhetorical forms and topics as means to invention suggests that there might be similar forms and topics for social science invention. These would be lists of topics that could be applied to any argument at any point to generate new things to say. The idea is simple. You have a tried-and-true list of abstract categories or concepts, and when you find yourself running out of ideas about some aspect of social life, you go to the list and see what it suggests to you. The problem is that you must first get some good lists of categories or concepts to use as topics.

Bearing in mind the fate of these lists in ancient times (that is, people took them too seriously, and the lists got very boring), we are not going to be particularly worried about whether our lists are the right lists or the true lists. It doesn't matter whether they are justified ontologically or epistemologically or whatever. (I wasted at least two years of graduate school trying to decide on the "right" abstract concepts and came to no conclusion at all. What I *should* have thought about was which lists seemed more fruitful, not which were "right.")

Here I will mention four such topical lists—two classical and two modern—that I myself have often found useful: Aristotle's four causes, Kant's list of categories, Kenneth Burke's five keys of dramatism, and Charles Morris's three modes of language. There's no particular reason these should be your topics lists. Indeed, I've used other lists from time to time. But these happen to be the ones that have most often proved useful to me. They are also lists that have recurred in the works of many writers under many different labels. But let me reiterate that this is not necessarily because they are "right" (although it would be hard to come up with a concept of cause that didn't fit Aristotle's analysis one way or another.) Rather, it's because they are useful. They help us make quick switches in our intellectual attacks on problems. You have already been introduced to one of these lists, by the way; I used Morris's modes of language to organize the first chapter of this book.

A. *Aristotle's Four Causes*

I start with Aristotle's four causes. It's a simple list:

material cause
formal, or structural, cause
effective cause
final cause

When we say, "The Republicans lost the election because they lost the women's vote," we invoke material cause. In this case, something happens because of the social materials that went into making or unmaking it. Demography is par excellence the social science of material cause. It concerns numbers of people of varying types and the ways in which those differing numbers shape social life.

By contrast, we might say with Georg Simmel (1950) that all social groups with three members are inherently unbalanced, because two of the three always ally against the third (something those of us who were only children in two-parent homes know very well). Here we are saying something not about social material but about social structure. It is the shape of the triad that gives it its peculiar properties. This is *structural* cause.

Aristotle's *effective* cause is the most familiar of his four. The effective cause of something is what brings it about, what forces it to happen. So we say that a strike caused employer retaliation or that a newspaper caused a war. These are statements about a direct kind of forcing.

By contrast, *final* cause refers to the aims of events. When we say the cause of universities is the need for education, we are attributing the existence of universities to their final cause (which today we often call function, although that's not exactly what Aristotle meant). When we say the reason for pollution laws is the need for clean air, we speak of final cause. Note that a lobbying group is likely to be the *effective* cause of those laws, even as a configuration of larger political interests and oppositions is likely to be their *structural* cause. And the numbers and distribution of those interests are the laws' *material* cause. Every event has causes of all four kinds.

Another example can show how using the four-cause list helps us think up new questions to ask. Consider unemployment. One can think of unemployment in terms of its *material*. The unemployed: Who are they? What are they like? What kinds of qualities do they share? Does unemployment concern a kind of person or a transitory state for many different kinds of people? This is to think of unemployment demographically. Or one can think of unemployment in terms of its proximate, *effective causes*: How do layoffs work? Who decides who gets fired or laid off? What are the incentives for choosing unemployment? What are the economic forces driving lowered employment? Or one can view unemployment in terms of its *formal, structural* properties: Could it be the case that unemployment is a general structural quality of a certain production system and that merely random forces decide who in particular is unemployed and why? Or one can view unemployment *functionally*, asking whether it does something useful for somebody (for example, does it help employers by lowering wages for those remaining in jobs, because they can be threatened with unemployment if they complain?) and whether that somebody, directly or indirectly, maintains it because of this utility.

As you can see, the Aristotelian list is very useful. Time and again, you can come up with something new by switching to a new type of cause from the one that you are implicitly using. It's also true that you can often come up with something new by switching from one to another *logical* concept of cause, from *sufficient* cause (something sufficient to bring another thing about) to *necessary* cause (something without which another thing cannot occur) and vice versa. But the Aristotelian list is probably more useful, which perhaps explains why it reappears with so many different names and guises; it can always be used in a tight spot to come up with a new attack on a problem.

B. Kant's List of Categories

The Kantian categories, although much more abstract than Aristotle's four causes, are also a useful list of topics. Kant thought there were some basic frameworks through which all experience was filtered. There are twelve of these categories, and they make another useful list of aspects of a problem to think about. Kant organized them under four basic headings: quantity, quality, relation, and modality. In what follows, I give the categories commonsense meanings, not the formal philosophical ones Kant gave. Our aim is not to get Kant right but to make him useful for us.

Quantity
   unity
   plurality
   totality

Quality
reality
negation
limitation

Relation
substance/accidents
causality/dependence
reciprocity

Modality
possibility/impossibility
existence/nonexistence
necessity/contingency

The Kantian quantity categories are unity, plurality, and totality. These suggest a number of essential ways to rethink a research question. Unity raises the issue of the *units* of our analysis: What are they? Why? How are they unified? What, for example, is an occupation? It's obvious what holds doctors together as a unit, but what about physicians' assistants? what about janitors? waiters and waitresses? Are these really units?

Plurality raises all the concerns of *number*. Are there few or many units? Does it matter how many there are? Could different people count them differently? So, for example, how many occupations are there? Does it make a difference whether we lump wait staff and cooks together? What about baby-sitters and elder-care workers? Or social classes: how many of them are there?

Totality raises the problems of the *overall nature* of a subject. Is it a unified whole? How would we know? In what ways is it divisible or indivisible? Social class is a famous example here. Is there a power elite, as C. Wright Mills thought? How unified are elites and ruling classes? Are social classes unified wholes or loose units that fade continuously into one another?

The Kantian quality categories are reality, negation, and limitation. These, too, suggest important ways to change our first conceptions of a research problem. The reality category raises the subtle but important question of *reification*, of mistaking an abstraction for a reality or—what is very common in bad social science thinking—imagining that because we have a name for something, it is therefore real. Take the famous concept of socialization, which is supposed to refer to all the training by which an infant and, later, a child becomes an adult. It is by no means apparent that this word refers to anything other than the sum total of experiences a young human has. Put another way, it isn't clear what experience a young person has that could not be said to be socializing that person for something or other. Nor is it apparent when socialization stops and life begins. There is in fact absolutely nothing that is denoted specifically by this concept; it is simply a reification following from the (fallacious) functional argument that because people acquire skills, there must be some special process—different from the rest of life—that "trains" them. Thus, the reality category invokes for us a crucial heuristic discipline, forcing us to ask whether the nouns we use in social science refer to real things.

Negation, too, is a centrally important topic. I shall later discuss several heuristics based on negation: problematizing the obvious, reversal, and the like. I shall also discuss the central heuristic importance of making sure that your idea is capable of being wrong. We should never forget to think about negation.

Finally, limitation is a crucial heuristic tool. Much of normal science actually takes the form of *setting limits* to generalizations, exploring what sociological positivists like to call scope conditions. Under what conditions is some argument true? At what times do certain forces take effect? These and a hundred other questions all arise from thinking about limitation. So, for example, we might find that many things that we think are long-standing traditions are in fact invented at particular moments. Under what conditions do people invent traditions: When their nationhood is threatened? When a nation is newly formed? Are there particular kinds of people who are more likely than others to invent traditions? Are they leaders of social movements? fallen aristocrats? Are there ways to differentiate invented and "real" traditions? All of these questions arise when we try to set limits on the concept of invented tradition.

The Kantian relational categories are even more important, and all have famous lineages in philosophy. The first of them is substance/accidents—the division of the world into given things (substance) and the properties of those things (accidents). In some parts of social science, the substance/accidents category provides no useful basis for heuristics. When we say that a person is a certain age, for example, we know very well that the person is the substance and the age is the property. But if I ask myself what, say, sociology is, it is not at all clear (unless I fall into reification) what the substance is and what the accidents. Is sociology a name for everybody with certain kinds of degrees and training? Then education defines the substance of sociology, and other things—people's political values, types of employment, sociological ideas and concepts—become accidents. But I could just as easily define sociology as people who hold certain kinds of jobs, in which case the jobs define substance, and political values, sociological ideas and concepts, and education itself become accidents. Note that this kind of analysis begins to suggest that the whole distinction of substance and accidents is probably a mistake (as, indeed, a large body of social theory believes). At the very least, reflecting on substance and accidents can help you change your way of seeing something.

The second of the relational categories is causality/dependence. Causal questions are obviously central to any heuristic, as we have seen in Aristotle's celebrated list of causes. I won't consider causality further here but simply refer the reader back to that discussion.

The third relational category is reciprocity. This, too, provides a helpful way to rethink social scientific questions. Often we find ourselves in a cul-de-sac, trying to decide which of two things causes the other. We know that higher levels of education are associated with higher income, but which causes which? Higher levels of education lead to higher income over the course of life, but availability of higher income allows the transmission of educational advantage across generations. There is a kind of reciprocity here between income and education that forces us to be much more specific about whose income, whose education, and what temporal orders are involved. The category of reciprocity reminds us to consider such chicken-and-egg models. Many, many systems in social life take this circular format of reciprocal causality. They can be self-reinforcing systems that stabilize themselves, or they can be runaway systems that blow up. (Loosely speaking, one arises from positive feedback, the other from negative.) The reciprocity category reminds us to think deeply about such systems.

Finally, the Kantian categories of modality are possibility/ impossibility, existence/nonexistence, and necessity/contingency. Possibility reminds us that it is easy to come up with social science arguments that are impossible and that, therefore, we need to check our ideas constantly for possibility. This is particularly true because much social science is motivated by a desire to improve society. But certain kinds of improvements are logically impossible. It is impossible, for example, for everyone to be successful if being successful entails some form of superiority to others. At least it is impossible unless we define all forms of success as being absolutely idiosyncratic. Yet social science is filled with arguments that implicitly believe everyone can be successful. So we must always reflect on the range of possibility in constructing our arguments.

The category of existence raises questions much like those of the category of reality. There are many types of social actors: doctors, left-handed people, the insane, and so on. Which of these types actually have existence as groups rather than as simple types? Indeed, what does it mean to say "have existence as groups"? There are many famous examples of this set of heuristic problems. It is easy, for example, to talk about class. But do classes exist? And what does it mean to say that classes exist? Are we talking about self-consciousness of class? about coordinated action? about simple common experience? Or take occupations. Are they simple categories of people? bodies of work? organized associations of workers? What does it mean to say that an occupation exists? Clearly the most famous examples of contemporary social science involve gender and race. Are women a group? In what sense? The heuristic questions raised by the category of existence are thus like those of the reality category. They lie in questioning nouns we commonly use to denote social groups and asking what kinds of things those nouns actually label.

Finally, the category of necessity/contingency raises obvious heuristic questions about how events relate to one another. In one sense, these are like the questions of the limitation heuristic: are certain relationships necessary, or are they contingent on other things (that is, limited)? But contingency is a much more complex phenomenon than mere limitation. It invites us to ask about the multiple dependencies among social processes, about the many paths that social processes can take. And necessity invites us to focus on necessary causality and its implications. When half the young men of England, France, and Germany disappeared in the trenches of World War I, a generation of young women couldn't marry—because there was no one alive for them to marry. The resultant family structure and indeed the resultant larger social structures of employment and opportunity shaped European society for generations. Like contingency, necessity pervades the social process. A good list of heuristics will never omit it.

The Kantian categories thus provide another useful list of heuristics. As with Aristotle's four causes, we can let the philosophers worry about the philosophical validity of this list. For us it is a useful checklist of things to think about. As it happens, Aristotle had a category list, too, which cut up the world a little differently. Aristotle included two things that

Kant made separate: space and time. Both of these are themselves useful heuristic reminders. Always ask yourself what the spatial and temporal settings of your problem are. How can they be changed? Which aspects of them are necessary or sufficient to determine which parts of the problem? Are there regularities to your question in space (either social or geographical) or time?

C. Burke's Five Keys of Dramatism

Moving to the modern setting brings us to the five keys of dramatism set forth by the famous literary critic Kenneth Burke in his book *A Grammar of Motives*: action, actor, agent, setting, purpose. We can use this list, too, as a heuristic aid to rethinking any particular problem.

Since this is a modern list, I can give a famous example. In his splendid book *The Culture of Public Problems*, Joseph Gusfield reconceptualized drunk driving. He said (among many other things) that accidents caused by drunk drivers are really a transportation problem, a problem of the *setting*, the locations where people drink. The San Diego police had consulted Gusfield about a sudden rise in accidents involving alcohol. He pointed out that if you built four major hotels on vacant land near interstate highways, all of them filled with bars and all of them inaccessible by foot, it was pretty likely that you were going to see more automobile accidents involving alcohol. If people get drunk where they can walk home (as in the pub in England), they are much less likely to drive drunk.

Behind this intellectual trick lay an analysis of alcohol-based accidents in terms of Burke's five keys of dramatism: Are fatal accidents best understood as a matter of *action*—driving a certain way, doing (or not doing) certain things (like fastening seat belts)

agents—certain kinds of actors (It turned out plenty of older drivers were drunk on the road, but they were less likely to get into accidents, possibly because they had more experience driving drunk and so were more skilled at it.)

scene—where people drink, how they get there, and how they leave (This was Gusfield's way of attacking the question.)

agency—vehicles and roads (If cars wouldn't move unless seat belts were fastened around passengers, fatalities would be reduced.)

purpose—why people decide to drive when, where, and how they do (Some people drive to get somewhere; others— young men, for example—drive to show off . . .)

Another excellent example of Burkean thinking is the famous paper of Lawrence Cohen and Marcus Felson that introduced the so-called routine-activities theory of crime (1979). Prior theorists of crime had emphasized criminals (that is, positive actors) as the key to crime. Cohen and Felson noted that crime takes three things: an actor (this had been the focus of prior research), a target, and an absence of guardians. We can think of an unguarded target as a certain kind of scene in Burkean terms. The central thrust of Cohen and Felson's argument is that changes in scene caused the crime increase after 1960. More consumer goods were in the home, they were lighter in proportion to their value (and hence more portable), and the entry of women into the labor force meant fewer people were at home to watch over property. The authors actually compared the weight of dozens of goods in Sears, Roebuck catalogs over the years, as well as the percentages of homes with no one home the first day the census taker called in 1960 and 1971. These and many other equally curious factors paralleled the huge increase in property crime from 1950 to 1975. Once again, a Burkean move raised a whole new theory, in this case of the sources and causes of criminality.

Burke's list is really just another version of the famous old reporters' list of topics: Who? What? Where? When? How? Why? And one can also see in it a fairly strong echo of Aristotle's four causes. Remember that the utility of all of these lists lies less in their novelty than in their heuristic power. Reporters use the who-what-when list to remind themselves to touch all the bases. We are more interested in using lists to remind us that our theories often focus excessively on one or another aspect of what we study. When we need to think anew, it's usually a question of figuring out what aspect of our analysis could be changed to produce a whole new view.

D. Morris's Three Modes of Language

A final topics list is Charles Morris's three aspects of symbolic systems: syntactic, semantic, and pragmatic. This list was of course used in Chapter One. Syntactic relations are relations between elements of the system. Semantic relations are relations between system elements and things to which they refer. Pragmatic relations are relations between symbolic statements and the context of action in which they are made. What is radical about my argument in Chapter One is its noting that many of my colleagues believe that pragmatic approaches to explanation are the only "real" ones. I used the Morris triad to start us thinking about explanation more broadly than is customary. That is, I used the Morris argument heuristically.

It can of course be used in other contexts. There is no necessary reason, for example, to think that it applies only to symbolic systems. You could think about the syntax of markets (internal market relationships) over against the semantics of the connections between groups in the market and their existence outside it. And you could go on to think about what actors in markets are doing (saying) and what the actions (the pragmatic context) of those market assertions are. One way of stating Marx's analysis of work is to say that there was a fundamental error in the belief of liberal economic theory in the separability of the syntax of markets (that is, the wage relationship) and the semantics of the social groups in those markets (workers and capitalists as they were outside the market). Liberal theory said these things could be separated; Marx showed, in endless empirical detail, that they could not. Maybe this is far-fetched, but seeing market relations as related to social relations outside production in the same way linguistic syntax is related to meaning and reference makes the traditional analysis of work suddenly look alive. We can think of new questions to ask.

WITH THE MORRIS LIST, I come to the end of my own current set of topical lists. Social scientists use many such lists through their careers. I have often used knowledge, feeling, action (from Plato, Aristotle, Kant, and any number of others) as a useful commonplace list. Many of us have used various lists of social functions—Talcott Parsons's adaptation, goal attainment, integration, and pattern maintenance, for example. Most of us also use the disciplines from time to time as a commonplace list: What will the economists think? What would an anthropologist say? Sometimes there's no faster way to come up with a new idea than to wonder how somebody from a different discipline would think about your issue. This is particularly so because, as I noted in the preceding chapter, academic disciplines are organized around different dimensions of difference.

The reader will want to use these and many other lists. But in closing my discussion of topics and commonplace lists, I want to underscore two cautions. First, do not reify these lists. Despite the philosophical fame attached to some of them, we don't need to assume their correctness or truth. They are simply useful lists of reminders of things to think about, reminders to use when you get stuck. Don't worry about their reality or truth.

Second, don't overuse them. Classical rhetoric died because students began to treat it as a meat grinder. So everything from tenderloins to rib eyes to pure gristle was turned into ground beef. Don't use these lists as some kind of comprehensive system that you put each of your research questions through. Just use them when you get stuck. Use them to stimulate your thinking. When you find that stimulation, turn to working out the details of the new argument. Don't run through every last heuristic list for every last idea and then try to put everything together. You'll never get anywhere.

Put another way, a little heuristic goes a long way. You are far better off making one major leap and then working out all the details and subparts of that leap than you are trying to work out the myriad minor leaps and subleaps that could be taken. Take the time to work out the details of a major heuristic move. As we shall see in the next chapter, most brilliant articles and books are built on *one particular move*. The author made a big move, then spent a lot of time working out the details.

GENERAL HEURISTICS
Search and Argument

CHAPTERS FOUR AND FIVE DESCRIBE general rules for coming up with new ideas. I shall illustrate these heuristics with a variety of examples drawn from several disciplines. The examples are illustrative, not definitive. The reader should not get the idea that a particular example illustrates one and only one heuristic. In fact, I end up reusing some examples. Just as there are several ways to think about any given method, there may be several ways to interpret the intellectual moves of any given article or book.

I shall also use some examples that were perceived as clever only a long time after they were written. Such papers are curiously common in the social sciences. The economist Ronald Coase's celebrated paper on the nature of the firm was published in the 1930s but did not become a touchstone of modern economics until the 1970s. (Coase won the Nobel Prize in 1991.) The anthropologist Fredrik Barth's *Models of Social Organization* was published in 1966 but didn't become a classic citation until much later. Ludwik Fleck's pioneering book on scientific thought styles lay fallow from its publication in 1935 until it was repopularized by Kuhn in the 1960s and finally translated into English in 1979.

That people took so long to recognize the creativity of these works perhaps tells us something important about the nature of creativity. Much of it has to do with how one's ideas fit with others' current beliefs. Creativity is *relational*. Coase's work went unappreciated until the rest of the economics community came around to the broad conception of economic thinking that Coase took for granted. Fleck's book was completely ignored until Kuhn's *Structure of Scientific Revolutions* prepared people for it. Often a mainstream cannot see new ideas as creative. Often it cannot see them at all.

This tells us about an important limitation on the practice of heuristic. You can easily be too radical for an audience. If you aim to have an impact, you have to adjust your heuristic gambits to your audience—whether it is a bunch of college friends, a seminar, or a subdiscipline. Note also that the cyclical relations among methods and the fractal character of social scientific debates mean that it is quite possible to be too radical for one group while being insufficiently radical for another. Practitioners of SCA might find Fleck's view of the conditionality of facts so radical as to be irrelevant, while contemporary sociologists of science would find him tame.

This rule—be different but not *too* different—takes us back to some earlier themes. As I said in Chapter One, the aim of social science is to say something interesting—perhaps even true—about social reality. We have some conventional ways to do that, which we call methods. The rule to be different but not too different reminds us that each methodological community has its own sense of how far is too far. It changes from time to time, of course. Many sociologists my age remember well the kid gloves with which we handled multiple regression in the 1960s, before it could be done in nanoseconds by eleven-year-olds. We always tested for interaction; we always repooled variances. No such care exists today. There are, however, *newer* rules about what's OK.

The heuristics in this book will sometimes take you clean out of whatever standard world you're currently in. That's the fun of it, as far as I'm concerned. But you should be advised that once you're outside the usual methodological communities, there are a lot of things that make strange noises in the social scientific night. That's why methodological communities and the addition heuristic exist—so you won't have to deal with those things on a regular basis if you don't want to.

In this chapter and the next, I discuss general heuristics. Unlike those in Chapter Six, these do not derive directly from the fractal debates of Chapter Two. They are tested ways of broadening what you are doing, ways to come up with new ideas, new methods, or new data, ways to get unstuck. Remember that these are not specifically aimed at any particular phase or aspect of the research process. They are useful at various times and in various ways.

I will discuss two kinds of general heuristic gambits in this chapter. The first are search heuristics, the simplest form of general heuristic. They involve seeking out new data, methods, and ideas. They are the first step beyond the additive heuristics of the preceding chapter. The second are argument heuristics. These are ways to play with or pose arguments in order to create openings for ideas. Like search heuristics, argument heuristics are general strategies for producing new ideas. But rather than helping you look outside your problem or data or way of thinking, argument heuristics help you look within, bending what you have into new shapes and new uses.

I. SEARCH HEURISTICS

Search heuristics are ways of getting new ideas from elsewhere. When you use search gambits as heuristics, you are betting that someone else has already thought seriously about your problem or something like it and that you can borrow that thinking. The central search heuristic is analogy. It could be an analogy about data: "the marriages I am studying are really like negotiations in business." Or it could be an analogy about a problem: "the problem of trying to explain why unions fail is just like the problem of trying to explain why X-ray machines fail." Note that in the second case, we aren't saying that unions are like X-ray machines, only that the process of failure has a certain logic to it in any circumstance.

A specialized but important search heuristic is the borrowing of methods. Borrowing usually involves analogy but goes beyond it to invoke not only some ideas but also a whole apparatus of analysis. It can be quite general or narrowly specific. Let us now look at these two search heuristics in detail, with some famous examples.

A. Making an Analogy

The first and in many ways most important of the general heuristics is making an analogy: saying that an X is really a G. (See? I surprised you—you were expecting Y. That would have come next if I were using the *additive* heuristic.) Examples of analogy are common in creative social science. Applying rational-choice models to explain state formation in feudal times means making an analogy between feudal kings and modern rational actors. Applying ecological models to humans—Park and Burgess applied them to cities in 1925, and Hannan and Freeman applied them to organizations in 1977—means making an analogy between human societies and biological systems. Applying economic models to family planning means making an analogy between people having children and people buying hamburgers.

These may seem like far-fetched analogies, but they were very productive. Consider the "economic" analogy. Gary Becker, the greatest apostle of this analogy, began his career with what was at the time a truly astonishing book, *The Economics of Discrimination*. Suppose, Becker said, we think about racial discrimination as basically an economic phenomenon. We can estimate a "price" of discrimination by the following method: We compare the hourly wages paid in southern textile mills that employ all-white labor forces with wages paid in mills employing mixed or all-black labor forces. The difference will be the price the factory owner is willing to pay for his discrimination, as if he were buying it like a suit of clothes. We can then bring all the apparatus of microeconomics to bear on that price, analyzing how it fluctuates with labor demand and supply, studying the trade-off between spending one's money on discrimination versus spending it on other things (new capital for the plant, for example), and so on. Becker's analogy must have seemed shattering at the time. Indeed, nobody outside the economics profession paid a lot of attention to *The Economics of Discrimination*. But the analogy was powerful, and when Becker began to analyze more mainstream topics, like family-planning decisions, his work began to be regarded as truly revolutionary.

Analogy is fundamentally different from addition. It means truly changing the terms of analysis, not simply adding something to them. It has a risk to it: there will be naysayers. At the same time, it can be very productive.

Many analogies take the form of Becker's, which begins with the theory and method and moves toward the data. The Becker claim was really "You may think that phenomenon X cannot be analyzed with my theory/method T, but in fact you're wrong: it *can* be." It is equally common for people to start from the data and use analogy to find new theories and methods. That was the source of the ecology analogies mentioned above. Park and Burgess looked at the raw complexity of the city of Chicago and asked whether the city looked like something that someone else had already come to understand. The answer was that it looked like the thing biologists call an ecology. So one way to understand it was simply to borrow the language and some of the analytic machinery thought up by biologists to analyze complex natural systems: the city is an ecology. Ditto for Hannan and Freeman, with their ecological approach to organizations. Organizational fields, too, can be seen as ecologies.

Looking for analogies from the data end is the more common experience for students. Suppose you are interested in the way cities are governed. The usual line of analysis treats this problem quite traditionally, as a question of understanding politics: voting, councils, bureaucracies. But it is perfectly possible to treat city government completely as a problem of economies: economies of favors, economies of patronage and politics, economies of location. In this analogy, city politics becomes simply an economy, and you can apply to favors, patronage, and decision-making all the machinery of economics: supply and demand, trade-offs, budget constraints, elasticity, and so on. You may not end up writing the final paper using the economic language, but under whatever surface rhetoric you *do* use, you can employ the borrowed arguments and ideas to understand things that may seem puzzling when you think of them purely in traditional terms as problems of power, authority, and influence. As this example makes clear, one of the useful aspects of analogy is that most often the ideas you borrow will be quite well worked out. When you forage in other disciplines and subdisciplines, you will find the intellectual supplies plentiful and well kept, ripe for the taking.

Analogies don't always work, not even the ones that make it into print. In two essays, the famous sociologist Talcott Parsons once gave an analysis of power and force in economic terms (1967a,b). He treated power as a medium of exchange, exactly like money. He treated force as the "gold" backing up the power ("money") system. He reflected on the uses of embodied power ("capital") to produce political growth (exactly analogous to economic growth). All of this hinged on a simple, direct analogy between power and money.

The two papers carrying out that analogy are brilliant but somewhat bizarre. They are brilliant because they make us think about power in a completely new way. They are bizarre because Parsons never used the analogy to question the distribution of power to individuals. Yet this is the basic topic of politics—who gets what where, how, and why?—though not that of economics (other than Marxian economics). This example teaches another useful lesson: in analogy, something centrally important can be lost—in addition to the something gained—unless we are very careful.

Note that analogy is not simply a matter of going to other disciplines and other bodies of knowledge. It is first and foremost having the ability to break out of the standard frames we put around phenomena. Having this ability means seeing, for example, that there is a close similarity between schools, prisons, and mental hospitals (David Rothman, *The Discovery of the Asylum*); that bodily fluids like mucus and semen cross boundaries in the same way unclassifiable objects do (Mary Douglas, *Purity and Danger*); that everyday interaction can be treated as drama (Erving Goffman, *The Presentation of Self in Everyday Life*). Obviously, it is crucial to know when and how an analogy works; after all, many people besides Goffman have seen life as drama, not least among them William Shakespeare. Often the key to an analogy is not having it but being willing to work out the details, which is exactly what Goffman did.

To cultivate analogy, you must do two things. First, you have to be willing to make rash connections. This willingness is itself a character trait, and you will need to get a sense of whether you are more or less analogical than others. If you have too little analogical power, you need to cultivate it; if too much, you may need to restrain it. But to use analogy effectively, you must have not only the character but also the means.

You must read broadly in social science and beyond. The more you have to draw on, the better. That is why many great social scientists are part-time dilettantes, always reading outside their fields, always dredging things up from some old high school or college course and putting them to new uses. (It's also one of the reasons why many great social scientists began life as historians, physicists, chemical engineers, literary critics, and even generals or lawyers.)

Of course, as I noted, the origins of analogies are generally well concealed by those who use them. And analogy often provides only the starting point for an argument, which must then be carefully elaborated and critically worked out on its own. But the overall fact is that many an influential paper has its roots in a fairly simple analogy that is carefully worked out. The pervasiveness of analogy is quite evident in famous titles and catch phrases like "economy of favors," "vocabularies of motive," "politics of knowledge," and so on, each one of which flaunts the analogy involved. Analogy is the queen of heuristics.

B. Borrowing a Method

Often there is a subterranean force driving analogy. That force is the desire to borrow (use, steal) a method. Students generally avoid borrowing. They feel that they are learning the methods of this or that field and that their faculty supervisors will expect them to use the local methods. Certainly in methods courses, that's true enough. But for the more general course paper and certainly for research papers and professional work, borrowing is often a smart thing to do.

Typically the borrowing relation can be put simply: "if only I could make an analogy between X and G, I could use all those methods people have invented for analyzing G." Sometimes these are quite general borrowings. Most of the statistical tools in SCA were borrowed in toto from biology and (later) econometrics (which got most of them from biology in any case). Correlational analysis, multiple regression, experimental and quasi-experimental design, hypothesis testing—nearly all were developed to analyze crops and fields and fertilizers and genetics. Other techniques came from elsewhere. The durational methods used by social scientists to analyze how long things take to happen (how long until a certain kind of law gets passed, how long until a given company folds) were developed to investigate the failure of industrial devices and the survival of sick patients. At the other end of the social sciences, much of anthropology, particularly since Clifford Geertz's famous methodological essay "Thick Description," has borrowed heavily from the textual-analysis methods developed by generations of literary critics.

Often, however, the borrowings are more specific and rest on contested analogies. I am responsible for one such borrowing myself. In the early 1980s, I realized that one could think of occupational careers—one of the most basic things to be explained in all of sociology—as simple sequences of events. I reasoned that if they were simple sequences, one could apply "sequencing" methods to them, and I had heard about the new computer algorithms just then being developed by computer scientists, cryptographers, and biologists to compare files, ransack code systems, and comb protein databases. Why not apply these to social data?

This idea proved quite powerful and spawned a mini-industry. But I had lost something important in the analogy.

The sequences in biology and computer science were not generated in a particular direction, as careers are generated in time. Surely the early stages of a career are more important in some sense than the later ones (because they can dominate where one ends up). The methods I borrowed did nothing with that importance. So the analogy had its weak side as well as its strong one, and the borrowing was consequently not a complete success.[1]

Like analogy, borrowing rests above all on a wide command of methods in one's own and other disciplines. It is by freeing oneself from the conventional association of certain objects of analysis with certain kinds of methods that one opens oneself to the rich possibilities of borrowing. But freeing oneself means nothing unless one has the knowledge, close or distant, accidental or carefully sought, of other methods and means of analysis. Analogizers and borrowers must always be reading and learning.

II. Argument Heuristics

Argument heuristics are ways of turning old and familiar arguments into new and creative ones. Search heuristics look elsewhere for ideas. Argument heuristics work with the ideas one already has, trying to make them look unfamiliar and strange.

The first argument heuristic is to problematize the obvious. For example, problematize the obvious notion that college is about learning things. Suppose the purpose of college isn't education at all. What else might it be? Indeed, is there any reason why college might be expected to have any purpose? Think of all the alternative reasons (other than education) for the existence of colleges, and make a decent case for each: saving parents' marriages by getting cranky adolescents out of the house, lowering unemployment by keeping millions of young people out of the labor market, providing a maximally supportive environment in which young people can experiment with erotic and emotional relationships, and so on. You will suddenly find that you know a lot more about the educational purposes of college as a result of this reflection. More important, now you can see the crucial questions about the *educational* purposes of college in a way that you couldn't before you thought about all the noneducational aspects of college. You have problematized the obvious.

A second argument heuristic is to make a reversal. Since everyone assumes universities educate students, assume they prevent education. List all the ways college life suppresses education: scheduling boring classes, providing differing individuals with uniform, uncustomized learning. There are dozens of ways—the nucleus of a good, contentious paper. Reversals are not necessarily reversals of truisms, however, although that is always a useful place to start. You can also just reverse phrases and ideas. I look at my bookshelf and see a copy of Edward Laumann and David Knoke's book *The Organizational State*. As I know well, the book tells how state actors (bureaucracies, boards, legislatures) are embedded in and surrounded by networks of organizations that seek to influence policies in various ways. But suppose I turned the title around and made *state* the adjective and *organization* the noun: *Statist Organization(s)*. What would such a book be about? Perhaps the ways in which organizations take on the properties of states—monopoly of force? Well, not real force, but perhaps economic force? bureaucracy? taxation? How can an organization be said to have citizens like a state? Now when I've gotten there—to citizens—I see that I have a topic. The waves of recent layoffs and the anguish of those laid off make it clear that for many people their work relationship does entail citizenship of a kind, with not only responsibilities to some organization but also rights in that organization. What kinds of organizations have citizens rather than employees? When in history have there been such organizations? How does the idea of employees' rights grow up? All of a sudden, I have the nucleus of a puzzle. Note, too, that I have drifted from reversal to analogy: the new title forced me to move the idea of citizenship to the world of organizations. But the starting point was a simple grammatical reversal: that's where I found the nucleus of the idea.

A third argument heuristic is to make an assumption—usually a rash one—and see what it gets you. The most familiar of these rash assumptions in social science is to assume that some actor or actors are "rational"; that assumption buys you all the methods of microeconomics and game theory. (It also has a contrary version: Herbert Simon's celebrated assumption that all rationality must be "bounded" in some way.) But you can assume plenty of other things. You can assume, for example, that because most human activities are conducted through language, language holds the key to all social explanation. One must therefore analyze it in any situation. This assumption led to exciting advances in the sociology of science, among other fields. As you can see, making an assumption is often a prelude to borrowing. You usually make an assumption in order to simplify or to translate.

A final important argument heuristic is reconceptualization, saying that what you thought was D is really E or even F. Suppose we reconceptualize college dating. Perhaps dating in college is not really about sexuality at all but about bragging rights. People date not because they are interested in intimacy but in order to prove something to people other than those they are dating. Therefore, dating should be categorized with other forms of bragging. Who knows if such an argument is true, but it suggests an interesting way of rethinking a familiar phenomenon.

Let us now consider these argument heuristics in more detail, using examples.

A. *Problematizing the Obvious*

Is there something everyone thinks is obviously true? A useful heuristic is to attack it systematically. Much of the time this gets nowhere; people are often right. But a substantial amount of the time, well-accepted and carefully tested ideas are profoundly wrong. They turn out to have been not carefully tested at all.

Perhaps the most famous recent example of this heuristic is *Time on the Cross* by Robert Fogel and Stanley Engerman. Fogel and Engerman attacked several widely accepted "facts": (1) southern slavery was dying as an economic system immediately before the Civil War, (2) slave agriculture was economically inefficient (and, consequently, defense of it was economically irrational), and (3) the southern economy as a whole was actually retarded by the existence of slavery. Fogel and Engerman rejected all of those propositions, which had been mainstays of the scholarly literature for many years when they wrote their book. In the process of that rejection, they demonstrated dozens of counterintuitive results: the money income of slaves in gang labor was higher than what it would have been had they been free sharecroppers (1974:1:239, 2:160); many large plantations had black management (1:212, 2:151); and so on. Fogel and Engerman's two-volume work caused a furor upon publication and for many years thereafter.

Fogel and Engerman were quite clear about problematizing the obvious. In fact, they devote many pages to explaining how a view of the economics of slavery that was so erroneous became standard. They also reveal (2: appendix A) that they were not the first problematizers of these "obvious" facts and point to the extraordinary difficulty such a heuristic sometimes faces.

Another fine example is Claude Fischer's *To Dwell among Friends*. Among the many truisms deflated by this book is the notion that people who live in cities are more isolated—have fewer friends and acqaintances—than people in small towns or rural settings. This belief is a staple of pop psychology and even of much serious scholarly work. Fischer went out and simply asked the question. It turns out that the truism was wrong, although, like many truisms, it contained a grain of truth in that the *kinds* of people urbanites know are somewhat different from those rural people know. They are more likely to be non-kin. But this turns out to be because urbanites are more likely to be young people, people looking for new opportunities and jobs, and so on. That is, people who are more likely to have networks full of non-kin are likely to live in cities *for other reasons*. Again, problematizing the obvious led to an exciting investigation, one that challenged old truisms and raised new questions.

A student doesn't need to take on so monumental a project as attacking truisms about slavery or the city. The world is littered with obvious facts that are wrong. Newspapers and magazines, with their strong interest in astonishing their readers, are fine sources of unsupported pieces of common sense: consider the beliefs that members of generation X hold certain attitudes or that the 1950s were particularly staid or that Americans are losing their belief in God or that the family is falling apart as a social institution. None of these has much truth in it, but all are standard fare in public discourse.

Social science is full of such hollow truisms, too. Take the common belief that social change is happening faster than ever before. It is not even clear what this means, much less that it is in any way true, yet it is a devout assumption of dozens of articles and papers. Or to consider something more controversial, take the idea that departures from equality in human systems need to be explained. This is a universal assumption of nearly all social scientific writing on inequality. We make this assumption every time we write articles on the causes of inequality across genders, races, classes, and so on. If inequality in these areas doesn't need to be explained, we don't need to write articles about it. Now, we might want to get rid of inequality for moral or political reasons, but why should we think it needs some special explanation? That is, why should we think it is unusual? We normally explain things that are unusual states of affairs, as I noted in Chapter One. Yet inequality, far from being unusual, seems to be nearly universal in human systems. If something is universal, we have to think very differently about its causes than we would if it were some special state of affairs.

Or you can simply take something as a problem that no one else has treated as such. When Bruno Latour and Steve Woolgar did an ethnography of life in a scientific laboratory (1979), all of a sudden people realized that we had taken life in the lab to be obvious and unproblematic. Turning the weapons of ethnography on it made it suddenly new and strange.

Problematizing the obvious grows out of the habit of always questioning things that are said or taken for granted. It's like a program running in the background on your computer. Every argument, every generalization, every background assumption that you run into, should be scanned with this simple check: Is that really true? Could I get somewhere by regarding this as a problem rather than as something taken for granted? The most extreme version of this scan is simply turning such arguments on their heads. That is the heuristic of reversal, to which I now turn.

B. Making a Reversal

Another of the central argument heuristics is to make a reversal. Sometimes this is simply a grammatical reversal. I was once asked to write a paper for a special journal issue on the subject of boundaries. Boundaries and boundary crossing had become very fashionable, so I was bored with the idea. "Boundaries, boundaries of things, of boundaries of things, of boundaries of things," I sang to myself in the shower one day. Suddenly, the commas moved, and I had the phrase "things of boundaries." What could that mean? I puzzled over it (after I got out of the shower) and tried to give it a real sense. Maybe social things like professions (groups I've spent much of my life studying) are "created" out of boundaries. The edges come first, then the thing, as if we created nations by having a border with place A and another discontinuous border with place B, and yet another with C, and so on, and then we hooked them up to make something continuous, and all of a sudden there was an inside and an outside, and we called the inside a nation.

The resulting paper—titled "Things of Boundaries," of course—grew out of that simple reversal. I made up the phrase, then tried to think of phenomena that fit it. Often reversal is not such a simple grammatical move but rather a reversal of some standard theory. Among the most famous examples of this is Howard Becker's paper "Becoming a Marihuana User," based on ethnography among marijuana users at a time when marijuana use was much less common than it is today. Becker started from the standard view of "deviant behavior": that certain people have propensities to do deviant things. In such a view, people take up pot smoking because of something characterological, a motivation to be deviant. Becker turned that idea on its head: "[I]nstead of deviant motives leading to deviant behavior, it is the other way around; the deviant behavior in time produces the deviant motivation" (1962:42). Becker's argument was that people had to learn to think of the loss of control and other physiological symptoms of getting high as *pleasant* experiences, rather than confusing or frightening ones. Hence, behavior came first and motivation—sometimes—afterward. This is precisely the reverse of our standard assumption about human behavior. That reversal opened up zones of investigation and possibilities of interpretation to Becker that had been closed to others.

Note that it is not necessarily clear, without talking to the authors who use this trick, whether the data forced it on them or it came to them in a flash, like my "things of boundaries" idea. But the best reversal papers combine data and interpretation in a way that seems magical. Mark Granovetter's

"Strength of Weak Ties" tells its reversal right in the title. Granovetter was interested in what makes interpersonal connections consequential. For years, scholars had drawn sociograms, diagrams with people as points and with lines between the points representing connections between people—connections by friendship, communication, exchange of money, or whatever. It was always loosely assumed that dense sociograms—sociograms in which most of someone's connections are also his or her connections' connections—are the strong type of network. What Granovetter noticed was that if we think about the *overall* degree of connection in a group that has several of these strong "cliques" as well as some links across the gaps between them, the nonclique ties (so-called weak ties) actually do most of the connecting. Because they were bridges between cliques, *overall* connection fell rapidly if they were taken away. By contrast, if any one tie within a clique disappeared, it didn't much matter, because the two individuals involved were probably connected through several other people as well.

Granovetter's empirical data involved finding employment. It turned out that the people Granovetter studied usually found jobs through some secondhand connection—a weak tie—rather than through an immediate friend. The key to employment was your distant friend's uncle's sister, not your best friend. Many people have had the experience of this kind of "accidental" job contact. And we all think of it as unusual. In fact, as Granovetter's theoretical argument shows, it's the common experience. Within our clique, all the people we know have the same job information we have because they are tied to the same people we are. It is through their friends *outside* the clique that new information comes in.

Another example is Paul DiMaggio and Walter Powell's famous paper "The Iron Cage Revisited," which was built on a direct challenge to the Hannan and Freeman paper I mentioned earlier (the one that borrowed ecology to study organizations). The central question of the Hannan and Freeman paper was why are there so many types of organizations? Their answer was that ecological forces produced differences. DiMaggio and Powell simply turned that question on its head. They asked, why do all organizations look alike? Obviously, on the empirical side, the two pairs of authors were looking to some extent at different aspects of organizations. But the fact remains that they used their different questions to make very different things out of what they *did* see in common. DiMaggio and Powell argued that only at the beginning of their lives were organizations subject to the ecological pressures for differentiation that Hannan and Freeman had seen. Afterward, they were pushed toward each other by forces of "isomorphism."

My interest here is not with the content of the DiMaggio and Powell paper but with the now familiar nature of its heuristic gambit. The paper turns the argument of another paper on its head, seeks a way to allow both to be right (by saying that ecological differentiation comes early in the lives of organization and isomorphism comes late), and then lays out a general theoretical argument about isomorphism and illustrates it with examples. Reduced to its barest form, it's just like Becker and Granovetter: "They've told you that X is true, but under certain conditions X is false. Let me tell you about those conditions." This is the simple reversal heuristic, and it produced—in the Becker, Granovetter, and DiMaggio and Powell papers—three of the most widely cited works in modern sociology.

My final example involves making a reversal in the data itself. Harrison White, a physicist turned sociologist, noticed that there are some mobility systems in which holes, rather than people, have the initiative (1970). No one can become president of Harvard until the current president resigns. Then somebody moves to Harvard to become president. This merely makes the hole—the vacancy—move to some other place. Then someone moves to fill *that* place, leaving a hole somewhere else. Eventually this "vacancy chain" gets to the edge of the system, and somebody enters academic administration from outside to fill the last slot. (Or perhaps the slot itself is abolished, ending the chain another way.) In such a system, *holes* have initiative. Nobody can move until a hole opens, and nobody can move exactly where he or she chooses; the possibilities are dictated by the holes that exist when an individual wants to move.

White saw that there was a whole class of occupations like this (football coaches, college presidents, Protestant clergy, company CEOs) and that there was a much larger class of mobility systems in which it was loosely true (university departments, law firms, hospital medical staffs). This insight turned our whole view of mobility on its head; it said that constraints were more important in mobility than either the choices or the character of those trying to move.

This reversal, like so many things, had its roots in analogy. In crystalline solids like semiconductors, there are electron holes, which are more or less negative electrons, absences that behave in most ways like electrons with positive rather than negative charge. So White the physicist already knew about a system in which holes played an important role. Perhaps the suggestion to make a reversal in the thinking about *people's* mobility simply worked its way out through his subconscious.

Like so many of my examples, the idea of vacancy chains is an example of several kinds of heuristics coming together. One of these is reversal—making holes more important than people. Another is analogy—between mobility systems and crystalline solids. The third is borrowing methods, for White turned his insight into empirical analysis by invoking a general class of probability methods (Markov models) well known (as of 1970) by physicists but unfamiliar to most sociologists.

C. Making an Assumption

Making an assumption—usually a simplifying assumption—can be a powerful heuristic. As I noted above, a simplifying assumption is often a step toward borrowing, usually from a discipline that analyzes simpler or more tractable systems. Thus, by assuming that "value" was a conservable substance like energy, economists were able to borrow the mathematical tools of statistical thermodynamics whole cloth (Mirowski 1989).

There are other reasons for making an assumption, besides adapting someone else's methods. Assumptions make for tractability; they make systems easier to think through. In formal demography, for example, it turns out to be useful to disregard men. As far as formal demographers are concerned, all men do is impregnate women; there are always plenty of men around to do that. It is the women who have the initiative; their age-specific fertility behavior determines the size and shape of a population. So demographers generally start from investiga-

tions of populations of one sex, assuming that women can determine their own fertility, getting pregnant if, and only if,
they please.

It is important to distinguish between such tractability assumptions, which are deliberately chosen, and background assumptions, which are merely implicit. All forms of analysis
have implicit assumptions. It is always a useful exercise to reflect on and question those assumptions. But I am here concerned with more conscious assumptions, which are designed
to open up a situation to analysis.

An excellent example of such an assumption comes in
Blau and Duncan's *American Occupational Structure*, already
mentioned in Chapter One as a classic example of SCA work.
Recall that the book analyzes the dependent variable of the
respondent's current job status by studying the way it is
affected by independent variables like father's job status,
respondent's education, and respondent's first job. When we
write an equation to estimate these effects, one thing we assume is that the causal pattern—the arrows describing what
affects what in the model—is the same for every case. This
translates into the assumption that every case follows the same
story.

Obviously this is a radical assumption. Otis Dudley Duncan, the methodological master who did the study, knew this
perfectly well. The idealized model order was father's job status
and father's education taken together lead to respondent's education, which leads to respondent's first-job status, which leads
to respondent's current-job status. Obviously, many cases will
reverse some of these steps. Men go back to school after starting work; men's fathers may make deliberate status sacrifices to

guarantee their sons' educations; and so on. But by making the radical assumption that the sequence was everywhere the same, Duncan was able to apply path-analytic regression and make some powerful guesses about the relative importance of all of these forces in shaping men's lives. The actual relationships were of course weaker than they seemed because they were conditional on an assumption known to be erroneous to some degree. But the power of the assumption was great, and the results, even though conditional, were worth the price.

Any strong assumption—like the Duncan assumption— creates the possibility of reversal. Although Duncan was well aware of his radical assumption, many of his followers lost sight of it. Obviously, a useful heuristic gambit is to challenge such a foundational but forgotten assumption. Peter Abell (1987) and I did exactly that with the Duncan assumption, insisting that we investigate the order of events in careers. The result: a variety of new concepts of career as well as new methods for analyzing narrative models for social life.

Another body of inquiry that was built on questioning a standard assumption is the bounded-rationality literature noted above. Starting in the early 1950s, the economist Herbert Simon challenged the idea that all economic actors are rational. In his book *Models of Man*, Simon argued that rationality was bounded—because there are costs to the information one needs to be rational, because the problems involved may be too difficult to solve, and so on. He proposed that people "satisficed" (from *satisfy* plus *suffice*); they make decisions by setting minimal thresholds for success and then search for actions only until they find one that beats the threshold. Later researchers have elaborated on this idea in dozens of ways.

Making and denying major assumptions thus constitutes another basic heuristic in the social sciences. Both moves produce challenging and surprising results.

D. Reconceptualizing

A final argument heuristic is reconceptualization. By this, I mean taking a familiar or taken-for-granted phenomenon and treating it as if it were an example of something quite different. Treat it not as a case of X but of Y or, even better, Z.

I gave in the preceding chapter the famous example of Joseph Gusfield's reconceptualization of drunk-driving accidents as a "setting" or location problem (too many people have to drive in order to drink in social places) rather than an actor problem (too many people are unable to control their cars because of alcohol intake—the concept implicit in the phrase "drunk-driving"). But automobile accidents had already provided a famous example of reconceptualization by a non–social scientist. Prior to the writings of Ralph Nader, it was thought that high speed "caused" accidents. Nader's book *Unsafe at Any Speed* reconceptualized injuries from automobile accidents; they were not a driver (agent) problem but a car (material) problem. Gusfield then later reconceptualized accidents involving alcohol as not a driver (agent) problem but as a location (place) problem. (Thus, both of these are based on moves in the Burke five-keys list of Chapter Three.)

Sometimes reconceptualization is almost forced on one by data. In the 1980s, some criminologists noticed that rates of motorcycle theft fell radically in states with compulsory-helmet laws (Mayhew, Clarke, and Eliot 1989). They saw a possible explanation for this if they reconceptualized motorcycle theft (and, later, most minor crime) as driven by opportunity; it was an opportunistic rather than a planned action. In a compulsory-helmet state, if you haven't got a helmet and you suddenly decide to steal a motorcycle, the police will stop you at once for the helmet violation and then figure out that you are a thief. The fact that motorcycle theft falls with compulsory-helmet laws makes immediate sense when you stop thinking of the crime as planned and start thinking of it as opportunistic. But the notion of opportunistic crime challenged long-standing "criminal personality" views of crime. Hence, the reconceptualization was a radical one.

Reconceptualization is always easier when one is working with the lists of topics or commonplaces I mentioned in the preceding chapter. A seasoned social scientist always keeps these kinds of lists in mind. He or she is always rethinking things of interest. Is my case really X or really Y? Can I say something new by recasting the whole framework within which I view my problem?

SEARCH AND ARGUMENT HEURISTICS are the simplest of the general heuristics. Analogy and borrowing, the major search heuristics, open to our use distant areas of investigation and thinking that aren't normally part of our repertoire. But as I noted, one can take advantage of these other areas only if one is aware of them in the first place. That's what makes insatiable reading and broad taste crucial to a good social scientist. They provide the basis on which search heuristics work. Argument heuristics, by contrast, make changes in what we already have at hand. Problematizing the obvious, making reversals, making assumptions, and reconceptualizing—these are all ways of taking what we already have and making it into something new and strange. Unlike analogy and borrowing, they aren't dependent on reading or breadth of knowledge. But they aren't dependent on depth of knowledge either. They are simply a matter of practice, of having the habit of doing them.

Note, too, that making assumptions differs from the other three argument heuristics. The other three are guaranteed to cause public notice. They explicitly change or challenge something. By contrast, making a big assumption is often something an author is conscious of but his or her followers are not. That certainly was the case with Duncan's assumption about uniform career sequences, although it was certainly *not* the case with Becker's assumptions about family-planning "rationality," which stayed controversial for a long time. It is probably the case that a good heuristic assumption is a radical one—one that gets noticed. Beware of assumptions that are mere conveniences.

Chapter Five
GENERAL HEURISTICS
DESCRIPTION AND NARRATION

I. DESCRIPTIVE HEURISTICS
  A. CHANGING CONTEXT
  B. CHANGING LEVELS
  C. SETTING CONDITIONS: LUMPING AND SPLITTING
II. NARRATIVE HEURISTICS
  A. STOPPING AND PUTTING IN MOTION
  B. TAKING AND LEAVING CONTINGENCY
  C. ANALYZING LATENT FUNCTIONS
  D. ANALYZING COUNTERFACTUALS

THE GENERAL HEURISTICS of the last chapter were largely concerned with the methods we use and our general conceptions of the objects of study. In this chapter, I will focus on how we actually imagine our object of study as something in the world, both at a moment and over time. Indeed, one could think of these as the heuristics of space and time. In the discussion of topics lists in Chapter Three, I mentioned the importance (in both Kant's and Aristotle's category lists) of space and time. This chapter recognizes that importance, suggesting some particular heuristic moves that have proved useful in recasting our conceptions of reality's layout in social space and of its flow through social time.

I. DESCRIPTIVE HEURISTICS

Descriptive heuristics have to do with how we imagine social reality itself. Description is not an innocent process. Every description has assumptions built into it, and challenging those assumptions is an easy way to produce new ideas.

First, a description always has a foreground and a background, a focal area and a context. So when we study industrial firms, for example, we take the economic conditions they face as context. We also think of the workers who work in them as part of their context, and we consider the local politics and schools in the towns where they are located as part of their context. When we study family dynamics, however, we take the industrial firms in which the family members work as context, as we do the schools and neighborhood in which family members study and live. There's no particular reason to make something part of the context rather than part of the focal area. The social process itself is completely continuous. But in order to cut down on the complexity of what we study, we make some things foreground and others background. Challenging these decisions is always an effective move.

Second, any description also has a "level," in the sense that there are things we imagine that are bigger than our object of study, things of which it is a part (and that possibly determine it), and things that are smaller than it, things it contains and in turn determines. An important heuristic move is to change this level of analysis, to decide that maybe the determining action takes place at a different level than we thought it did. Consider the subject of success in school. There is a long history of researchers' trying to decide whether the determining action takes place within individuals (differences in talent), within families (differences in family resources and values), or within school systems (differences in school resources for teaching). In this literature, the explicit question is the determining level of causality.

Finally, a description doesn't necessarily apply everywhere. Perhaps we want to limit the range of a description, to say it applies in some places but not others. Changing this range of application is another important heuristic, one that raises important and novel questions for analysis. Suppose, for example, we argue—as is commonly stated in various public media—that illegitimacy rates among African Americans are frighteningly high. An obvious heuristic for opening up this question to analysis is to ask where else that description might apply: among whites? Hispanics? the highly educated? and so on. (It turns out that illegitimacy rates are rising throughout the population as a whole.)

More generally, condition-setting concerns the question of "how big" the phenomenon of interest is. We might be studying the rise of professions in modern history, for example. But perhaps the rise and structuring of expert occupations are not really phenomena that happen in isolation but are part of a much larger movement regularizing and formalizing all sorts of behaviors: investment (formalized in accounting), law (in codification of laws), and even music (in the creation of the even-tempered scale). In that case, we *really* should be studying a broader phenomenon, called rationalization. (This was Max Weber's argument.)

A. *Changing Context*

Changing context is a powerful heuristic because it brings together things we have carefully set apart or it rearranges the
way we connect social things. I am not thinking here so much
of the idea that the context determines what happens. (I'll consider that next.) I am more concerned with simply rearranging
things on a given level, rearranging what is in our focus of attention and what is outside.

For example, suppose you are studying why students choose
to go to particular colleges. You gather material from college
view books, promotional materials, Web sites, and so on. You
study students' interests and search patterns. But you don't
find much. Students seem to apply to a strange variety of
schools: a mix of four-year colleges and universities, urban and
rural, famous and not so famous. Moreover, students seem to
respond to extremely minor differences between schools. How
about changing the context? Could it be that applying to and
considering colleges are really, at first, about staking out a position as a kind of person at home or in high school or among a
friendship group? That is, the context of the decision is not
simply the student in the abstract but the student as someone
who is trying to tell his parents that he is sensible or her
friends that she is daring or his school that he can run with the
best, and so on? This context narrows and changes as decision
time draws near and family economic and practical realities
loom. But the crucial issue is one of context. We change our
thinking about college applications by asking whether we have
the right context for the problem.

A splendid example of context changing is Arlie Hochschild's *The Managed Heart*. Hochschild's book puts together

two realms of investigation normally considered separate: emotions and work. Traditionally, studies of work treated emotional life as a *context* for understanding what goes on in the workplace. There had been a substantial literature on the "informal organization of the workplace" and whether it helped or hindered the organization. This literature saw friendship, personal rivalry, and so on as a part of the context of the formal structure of the organization, but no one had thought about emotions as part of the foreground, as part of work itself. Hochschild's decision to make emotions the foreground led her to the concept of "emotion work," work that involves changing one's own feelings in order to produce a "proper state of mind in others" (1983:7). It also led her to a remarkable study of the lives and experiences of people who do such emotion work (flight attendants, bill collectors, and others), which remains one of the most interesting pieces of sociology of the last quarter century. Bringing emotion to the foreground was a brilliant idea.

Changing context is a particularly powerful heuristic tool because contexts are usually established by largely conventional rules within disciplines and disciplinary subcommunities. In many ways, undergraduates are better positioned to change the contexts of their problems than faculty members are, because they don't know the conventional contexts assigned in the literature. It is always worthwhile to think about changing the context. Are there parts of your phenomenon that you are treating as background that could become foreground, or vice versa?

B. *Changing Levels*

When we think about some social phenomenon—work, say, or cities—we have a level at which we start thinking about it. Take the example of cities. When we ask what cities look like—how they are shaped, what kinds of people live where in them, and so on—our first inclination is to think at the level of the individual city. So we look at who doesn't like whom and who doesn't want to live next to whom and who moves where, when, and why. We look at transportation structures, land values, industries.

But it might well be that the structure of cities is mainly determined by some larger phenomenon, the national or global economic pattern, for example. This is the theme of Saskia Sassen's *The Global City*, which holds that the structure of certain "primate cities"—New York, London, Tokyo—is determined by their nature as centers for producer services (law, accounting, banking, insurance, and other services businesses need) in the global economy. This centrality generates a demand for certain kinds of employees, who in turn have certain kinds of incomes and tastes, which in turn generate a lot of follow-on markets and kinds of employment. That is, the producer-services industry thrives on concentration, which in turn dictates where producer-services employees live and what kinds of retail operations and services must be locally available. By implication, Sassen's argument (the dominance of the international division of labor) could be extended to other types of cities in a global economy.

In this argument, explaining a "lower-level" phenomenon can be a complete mistake. The real phenomenon of interest may be much larger and the lower-level one driven by the part it plays in the larger one. The same argument can of course be made in reverse. In a famous article on "The Cumulative Texture of Local Urban Culture," Gerald Suttles argued precisely the opposite of Sassen. Any city, he said, acquires over time certain political habits and rigidities. These will be in many ways unique, and they will overdetermine the fate of all sorts of urban change: political, cultural, even industrial. Chicago, with its relatively cohesive elite closely tied to an aging political machine, is quite different from multi-elite New York and more open and freewheeling Los Angeles. To see a single pattern in city politics is to look at too general a level. Not only should one not see particular cities as determined by global structure, one should also not believe in general patterns of city politics but only in a general process (aging) that produces unique patterns in each city.

What matters is not that one or the other of these arguments is right or wrong but rather that both of these works have become celebrated and fruitful foundations for further studies of urban life. Both led to extensive bodies of research because both invoke the important heuristic of changing levels.

Perhaps the most extraordinary example of such context changing in recent social science—the grandfather of all "globalization" arguments—is Fernand Braudel's monumental study *The Mediterranean*. Braudel argued that the "events" of the Mediterranean in the sixteenth century were just so much flotsam and jetsam on the surface of the sea. The nature of events was dictated by what he called conjuncture, a middle level of historical reality that included fluctuations in prices, changes in trade patterns, and developments in naval practice and power, in types of governments, and in forms of war. But beneath everything, like a steadying foundation, was "structure," the unchanging and determining basis of Mediterranean life. Structure began with the environment—geography, seas, islands, boundaries, climate—but also included foundational human practices: the nature of towns, nomadism and "transhumance" (regular long-distance migration and return), types of ships, and other such things. For Braudel, structure was the most important (about four hundred pages worth), conjuncture came second (about five hundred pages, but then conjunctural things changed, so they took more space). Events—the stuff of most histories—take only the last three hundred pages of Braudel's two volumes. The structural and conjunctural contexts determined them.

Braudel's book abounds in interesting heuristics. His upside-down map of Africa (showing "how the great Sahara desert dominates the sea" [1972:1:169] is a spectacular example of reversal. But his most extraordinary effect was to give rise to several generations of level-raising arguments, from the world-systems theory of the 1970s to the globalization theory of the 1990s. All of these result from Braudel's radical changing of level, his insistence that grand conjuncture above all drives the little events below.

C. Setting Conditions: Lumping and Splitting

Setting conditions is a matter of deciding where a particular description applies. Put another way, it is a matter of deciding whether to split some social phenomena apart or lump them together.

Thus, another way to think of what Sassen did in *The Global City* is to say that the book draws a distinction between the great producer-services cities—New York, Tokyo, and London—and all other urban places. Of course, the distinction was overdrawn. Many other cities partook of this or that characteristic of the global triumvirate. But precisely what made the book powerful and attractive heuristically was that drawing such a tight line around the phenomenon allowed Sassen to write about an extreme version of it. This in turn allowed her to explore the phenomenon of globalization at a depth that might not have been allowed had she analyzed a larger class of cities. Making a strong distinction allowed her to push an argument to the limit.

One could, by contrast, choose not to make a distinction but to lump things together as instances of a single phenomenon. Among the most celebrated examples of this in social science is Norbert Elias's *The Civilizing Process*. Elias took dozens of subjects that used to be separate—table manners, nose blowing, spitting, bedroom behavior, and so on—and assembled them into an image of private "civilization," which he then even more audaciously connected to the formation of modern states. All of these things together, he argued, constituted a grand "civilizing process." Like Braudel's "structure," Elias's civilizing process was a huge conception. But here the idea was not Braudel's of changing our idea of the determining level of a system but rather an argument that things we had thought utterly separate—the history of nose blowing and the history of the absolute state—were in fact part of one large process.

Again, there is no need for the student to be so audacious or grandiose. But it is often a useful heuristic to lump together things that others have left separate. Merely to propose such a lumping together is to raise a hundred interesting questions and issues for investigation.

So, too, one can split things apart. This is not the same as saying that the lower level is the determining one. Rather, it asserts that some regularity or description applies over a narrower range than we had thought. This has been the overwhelming strategy of writing about women for the last twenty years. For example, Cynthia Epstein's *Women in Law* makes the case that while there are already many books about lawyers, most of the generalizations in them don't apply to lawyers who are women. Splitting has been the order of the day in many fields: ethnic and racial studies, gender studies, and so on. Note, however, that it is a quite general heuristic move and has nothing inherent to do with activist research. Jerome Carlin's *Lawyers on Their Own* made precisely the same claim about lawyers in small, solo practices—that they were quite different from other lawyers—that Epstein made about women lawyers.

II. NARRATIVE HEURISTICS

Descriptive heuristics propose changes in the way reality is described. Narrative heuristics involve changing the way we use events and stories to think about social life. In this sense, Elias's "civilizing process" is as much a narrative move as it is a descriptive one. It weaves a number of separate narratives into one grand story. (This underscores an important point: it doesn't matter what we *call* the ways in which we generate new ideas just so long as we *have* new ideas.) There are four important narrative heuristics to discuss. The first two involve the degree to which narration enters our thinking about a problem:

whether we view processes dynamically or not and whether we focus on contingency.

An obvious first move is to take something that has been viewed statically and put it into motion or, conversely, to take something that has been seen narratively and make it static. As usual, there is no great issue of faith here. To those who are fascinated by the processual nature of social life (I'm one), it may seem crazy to treat freeze framing as a legitimate heuristic. But sometimes that's the best way to understand social life. Indeed, much of history works this way. Grand-narrative characterizations come apart on close inspection. For example, most histories of America speak of the 1920s as the Jazz Age, but on closer inspection—looked at in isolation—the 1920s seem extremely diverse. Conversely, many static interpretations become quite different when seen dynamically. Consider conditions in high-tech industries today. The senior managers of these companies view the situation more or less statically, within the narrow time frame of quarterly returns and stock market value. But the workers themselves experience their work within the longer, dynamic time frame of their careers. Depending on our research interest, we are going to want time to freeze or flow.

A second narrative heuristic involves contingency. Many social science models disregard contingencies. They are based on the belief that the same kinds of results can come about in several ways and that if we aren't specifically interested in the details of the pathways, we might as well disregard the contingencies that determine them. A rather interesting example of this comes from the literature on people's lives. A long-standing belief held that negative life events—sickness, bereavement, unemployment, and so on—could lead to various forms of distress. The surprise came when several writers proposed that positive life events—promotion, marriage, and so on—would have the same effect, something that turns out to be more or less true. Thus the contingency—distress came only if the life events were negative—turned out to be irrelevant. Sometimes contingency matters *less* than we think.

On the other hand, sometimes contingency is centrally important. Harrison White's vacancy-chain model, mentioned earlier, is an example of a completely contingent model, at least with respect to individuals' careers. The presence of such overwhelming contingency effects often means that we are working at the wrong level of analysis. White's model is ultimately a structural one, in which the larger system has dominance over local initiative.

A third narrative heuristic involves latent functions. Latent functions are unplanned or largely unnoticed results of social institutions or actions, which, however, turn out to be important. Indeed, it may be the case that these latent functions become more important than acknowledged functions. When I discussed problematizing the obvious, I used an implicit example of latent functions: the alternative purposes of college. Maybe college is not for education but for reducing unemployment by keeping many young people out of the full-time labor force. In that case, education is the ostensible function, unemployment the latent function. This particular example of problematizing the obvious worked by problematizing the ostensible function of an institution and looking for latent functions. There are many other things to problematize about college, of course: common beliefs about who goes there, what people actually do there all day (faculty do *not* teach all day, for example), and so on. But looking for latent functions is always a useful heuristic.

My final narrative heuristic is the counterfactual: what would have happened if . . . Some disciplines are particularly well set up for counterfactual analysis. Economics has a particular advantage here, because of its ability to "impute" prices to unpriced things by estimating the costs of the other things people forego to have the unpriced ones. But counterfactuals are also widely used in history. For example, the implicit counterfactual in A. J. P. Taylor's *Origins of the Second World War* (discussed in Chapter One) is that if Hitler had not invaded the Soviet Union and gratuitously declared war on the United States, he might have gotten away with most of his gains up to that point. The counterargument to *that*, however, is that he got the earlier gains by making precisely those kinds of audacious moves, but on a smaller scale. Someone who knew when to stop could never have made the earlier bold moves that got him to the point where he made his "mistake." Thus we see that the core of the argument about Taylor's thesis lies in the nature of Hitler's personality and the political system that allowed his personality such comprehensive sway in German policy. By thinking counterfactually, we see where the argument's hinges are.

Let us now examine these narrative gambits with more detailed examples.

A. *Stopping and Putting in Motion*
The first narrative heuristic involves history itself. If your present analytic strategy is static, how about making it dynamic? If

it's dynamic, how about making it static? As with so many heuristics, the question isn't whether the social world is in fact historical or not. You don't have to be Max Weber to know the answer to that question. But sometimes it's useful to *attend* to that history, and sometimes it isn't.

The more familiar move is from static to dynamic. Whenever we move to a new town or school, it seems fixed, a slice of time. Only after staying for a few years do we know which parts are changing and which stable. Theories we adopted at first seem silly once we understand that this or that part of the slice was in fact in rapid motion. Thus you might wonder why some favorite store leaves a mall to set up in a new location. You might develop a story about problems between the store and the mall, problems with competitors, and so on. But then if a new development springs up around the store's new location, you may suddenly realize that in fact your favorite store had been located in the original mall only temporarily, while its new quarters were being built. What seemed to be static turns out to have been in motion, but because you first got to know the store in its temporary location, you didn't see that.

One of the central difficulties of assessing any social situation at a single moment is precisely our inability to see the snapshot merely as part of a movie reel. This point is made with unerring accuracy in one of the most influential works of modern anthropology: *Political Systems of Highland Burma* by Edmund Leach. Leach set out to do "a functionalist study of a single community," the classic ethnographic slice of life. He was only a few months into the work when the Second World War turned Burma into a war zone. Shortly afterward, Leach entered the army and spent the next five years drifting in and out of northern Burma, visiting nearly every society in the area. Most of his field notes were destroyed in enemy action, and he wrote his great book from memory, his few surviving notes, and what published materials he could find.

Leach's central point was that the stability implied in the classic community studies was a mirage. In his characteristically blunt prose, he wrote:

> The generation of British anthropologists of which I am one has proudly proclaimed its belief in the irrelevance of history for the understanding of social organization. What is really meant by these arguments is not that history is irrelevant but that it is too difficult to put on paper. . . . Thus Professor Evans-Pritchard, who is one of the most staunch upholders of equilibrium analysis in British social anthropology, is also an advocate of the use of history in anthropological analysis, but he has not yet explained how the inconsistencies between the two positions can be resolved. (1964:282–83)

Leach was right about "history," of course. Often the best move possible is to put one's data in motion, to see long-run change rather than simple equilibrium. But having made that move, Leach himself made a quite peculiar reverse. He preserved equilibrium by saying that the ritual and symbolic systems of the Kachin act *as if* there were equilibrium societies in Burma. Their cultural system draws on a language of stability but uses that language to do "historical," changing things. The anthropologists' mistake, then, lies in taking the tribes' symbols for the reality. Curiously enough, Leach made the move into history and then took it back again. (This wading into the water and then hurrying back to shore seems to be common among anthropologists. Marshall Sahlins's influential *Islands of History* makes much the same move.)

From our point of view, what matters is the heuristic. Leach and Sahlins to some extent got caught up with the issue of whether the flow of events was really there, whether it did or didn't matter because there is an equilibrium. In some ways, Evans-Pritchard may have been better off. By trying to keep both sides—whatever the inconsistencies—he was testifying to the heuristic utility of invoking as well as ignoring the passage of time.

So, by contrast, sometimes we need not put our problem into motion but must stop the motion that is already there. Typically we want to do this when our interpretation of some particular moment is being driven more by the narrative in which we have embedded it than by things we actually know.

An excellent example of this is the magnificent historical ethnography *Montaillou: The Promised Land of Error* by Emmanuel Le Roy Ladurie. Throughout the course of modern scholarship, the heretic peasants of southern France had been perceived chiefly in their role as the last representatives of the Catharist (Albigensian) heresy. They are noticed in history mainly for the strangeness of their beliefs (the highest Catharist virtuosos, the perfecti, fasted completely—until death resulted—after their ceremony of "heretication") and for the brutal crusades that suppressed them. By provoking these crusades, these peasants played a central role in establishing the (northern) king of France's power in Languedoc, the southernmost part of what is now France. That is the usual story of the heretic peasants of southern France.

But the inquisition that rooted out the heresy kept detailed notes. And Le Roy Ladurie realized that one could read the inquisitorial records not so much as evidence about Catharism per se but as evidence about the community as a whole, about economy and residence, about family and marriage, about sheep and migration. Suddenly, Catharism becomes not something strange and perplexing but something deeply comprehensible in the context of the culture at the time. History thus becomes ethnography in this book; long-dead historical records give rise to a living, daily culture.

This practice of stopping the clock is an important one, and it is important not only in areas of historical inquiry. The move of stopping the clock is central to all forms of equilibrium analysis. Thus in many branches of economics, a market may be far from stable at any moment, but by analyzing its behavior in equilibrium, one can specify the direction of the forces playing upon it. So, too, in certain forms of game theory. Even extended games—games that take place as repeated plays over time—can sometimes be reduced to a strategic form, in which the answer is given at once, no matter how the repeated plays might get there in practice.

Stopping the clock essentially enables you to attend to more things in the present. It allows you to broaden the context, possibly to change levels. That is, it can be a gateway—like so many of these moves—to other heuristic moves. We often think reality is fundamentally historical. But it is still useful to imagine it, from time to time, as frozen for a moment. These can be big moments to be sure. When Braudel is justifying his concept of structure in *The Mediterranean*, he writes at one point: "[T]hat these two hundred years, 1450–1650, should form a coherent unit, at least in some respects, clearly demands some explanation" (1972:2:895). How can two centuries be a "moment"? Well, they can't, but by pretending that they are, we can open ourselves to some important insights.

B. Taking and Leaving Contingency

Contingency also produces an important heuristic. One can generate many new views of a theory or a regularity by arguing that it is contingent on something. Conversely, one can sometimes produce extraordinary results by disregarding contingency. The latter is, indeed, one of the standard moves made in formal and quantitative work.

As an example of taking contingency seriously, consider Michael Piore and Charles Sabel's argument in *The Second Industrial Divide* that there was nothing foreordained about mass production. According to their argument, modern economic growth might have been sustained by small, flexible production units. There was no absolute need for assembly lines and interchangeable parts. Piore and Sabel's controversial argument has spurred an enormous mass of research on those areas of the world (southwestern Germany and northern Italy, for example) where complex webs of flexible producers have indeed survived. A number of interesting consequences followed from the book. First, the book suggested investigating the web-like subcontractor structures, educational systems, and credit arrangements that *support* these industrial areas of "flexible specialization." That is, the book had direct consequences for industrial policy. Second, it suggested rethinking the old narrative of industrialization itself: Was the role of artisanal labor as tangential as it had been made to appear? What were the consequences of the "industrial divide" for the labor movement? On the one hand, "massification" created more powerful employers. On the other, it created conditions that made union recruitment easier. Suddenly, the history of modern work looked different.

By contrast, there are also arguments implying that perhaps contingency isn't as important as we think. Making an even stronger argument in his book *Normal Accidents*, Charles Perrow suggested that one could work out a relatively systematic theory for rare and contingent events, such as nuclear-plant accidents, ship collisions, and the like. The book opens with a thrilling, utterly contingent account of the Three Mile Island accident in 1979. Perrow then asks what kinds of factors allow contingency—in the sense of random probability—to dominate systems. He comes up with two. The first factor is the complexity of a system; complex systems have lots of feedback loops and lots of parts serving multiple functions, possibly in ambiguous or unmeasurable ways. The second factor is the coupling of the system; tightly coupled systems are strongly time dependent, with many invariant sequences of action in them and, typically, only one way of successfully operating. Perrow's basic theory is that normal accidents—that is, "systematically produced" contingent events—are most common in complex systems that are also tightly coupled systems. He thereby achieves something of a theory of contingency.

Considering the role of contingency is always important in thinking about social life. The heuristic moves of either invoking more contingency or ruling out contingency can often burst open an intractable problem. Suppose you are writing a term paper on medical paraprofessions like pharmacy, radiography, and nursing. You read books on each one, and it looks as though they are all getting more and more professional, taking over more and more functions. At the same time, they seem to be involved in lots of little fights with other paraprofessions or with medicine itself. That seems a rather flaccid, dull design for a paper: "professionalism is on the rise, but there is lots of squabbling." Is there a way to regard all of these little fights not as contingent but as systematic? By viewing the competitors all at once in a competitive field, you can see them as contesting a limited set of resources. As in White's vacancy chains, you may tame contingency by seeing it as the outcome of a structured system of competition. You have moved to a new level and can theorize an arena of competition within which these fights can be understood systematically.

C. Analyzing Latent Functions

Functional analysis has come into and gone out of fashion several times in the last half century. Functional arguments are elusive. Sometimes they seem to be simply elaborated versions of rational-choice arguments: function equals purpose equals something we choose to do. Sometimes they are purely logical in nature, as in the classic "imperative function" argument that since there are certain things that must occur for a society to work, we must (and can) always identify the social structures that make those things happen. (Sometimes such arguments are simply rationalizations for moral arguments about how society *ought* to be organized.)

The debate over functionalism is deep and complex, but I am interested in functional arguments merely as heuristics. Often we look at a social institution or structure and develop a theory of it based on what seem to us the obvious purposes or functions that it serves. But it may well be that there are *hidden* forces keeping it in place, either purposively or otherwise. Reflecting on latent functions can take us to these forces, which we can then analyze as we see fit.

An example of latent functional analysis is Richard Edwards's book *Contested Terrain*. Divested of its fairly strong political overlay (Edwards was a radical with a distinct point of view), the book's basic argument is that the usual history of employment relations in the United States got it all wrong. The traditional argument was that an "efficiency" movement dominated American labor relations for the early years of the twentieth century. This was "scientific management," with its stop watches, piece rates, stringent work rules, and so on: the world of work skewered by Charlie Chaplin in the film *Modern Times*. On the traditional interpretation, scientific management was driven by the engineering profession; the attempt to rationalize labor on the shop floor had grown out of rationalized production itself. In this story, scientific management was then replaced in the 1930s and after the war by the "human relations" school of management, with its much broader focus on workers' lives and happiness, welfare capitalism, and similar policies.

What Edwards pointed out was that although the human-relations school looked like a kinder, gentler form of management, in fact it concealed an enormous expansion of bureaucratic rules and regulations that vastly extended firms' control over workers' lives. He argued—quite persuasively—that the real purpose of both schools of management was to discipline the labor force. The surface, ostensible functions may have been hyperefficiency and "taking care of workers," respectively. But the latent function was the same in both cases: control of the workers.

It doesn't matter, for our purposes, whether that control was planned or accidental. The point is that the search for latent functions often turns up important social forces. I have several times mentioned the latent function of college in safeguarding employment opportunities for the larger labor force. This may seem an odd way to think, but in the years when American labor was dominated by industrial workers, organized labor strongly opposed any attempt to create the kind of combined apprenticeship-schooling system that trains much of the labor force in Germany. Such a system would, in fact, have threatened too many jobs. College's function of controlling unemployment may be more important than you think.

So latent functional analysis is always a useful strategy. You may turn up nothing at all. But you may turn up important things indeed.

D. Analyzing Counterfactuals

Finally, I wish to consider counterfactuals. One of the most useful narrative heuristics is *what if?* We are used to practicing this in our own lives, as in "If I hadn't gone hiking in Europe that summer, we wouldn't have met and gotten married." From the social science point of view, of course, there are hundreds, thousands, maybe even tens of thousands, of people to whom one could have been successfully married. Our lives might have differed in various ways, but most of them wouldn't have been very consequential—in terms, let's say, of our ultimate type of employment, our financial situation, or the socioeconomic status of our children. There is thus little general interest in investigating counterfactual might have beens, although there may be considerable personal interest in them.

Often, however, counterfactuals are vitally important. Would there have been something like a fascist Germany without Adolf Hitler? Would Chicago have become the major city of the Midwest if St. Louis had become a major rail hub? Would American history look fundamentally different if a watchman in the Watergate complex hadn't noticed that the latch was taped on a basement door in 1972?

Posing counterfactuals can be very productive. We often do it merely for the purpose of improving our case against them—that is, to improve the argument for what *did* happen. But sometimes—particularly in the 1960s and 1970s—counter-factual analysis has been an elaborately developed mode of analysis.

One of the most brilliant uses of counterfactual heuristic was Robert Fogel's *Railroads and American Economic Growth*. Fogel problematized the obvious "fact" that railroads were central to American economic growth. What would have happened, he wondered, if there had been no railroad? Obviously, there would have been *a lot* of canals. But what of the actual economic consequences? As Fogel pointed out, to a considerable extent the railroads were *given* their role flat-out; 30 percent of their total capitalization came from federal and state governments as gifts. Indeed, Fogel's introductory chapter is filled with such information, a brilliant use of familiar facts and simple economic theory to demolish what most of us accept as a truism.

Two hundred pages later, Fogel concludes that "no single innovation was vital for economic growth during the nineteenth century. . . . The railroad did not make an overwhelming contribution to the production potential of the economy" (1964:234–35). In between, those two hundred pages contain calculations of wagon-haulage distances in primary markets, studies of the impact of demand for rails on the American iron market, maps of canals that could have been built, and so on. The book is a tour de force, teaching us not only something important about a period but, much more important, teaching us something about the vulnerability of received and accepted ideas.

Few students will have the temerity and energy Fogel has displayed (and continues to display) over his career. But counterfactual thinking is always useful. Return to the example of marriage. If you could have been happy with any one of hundreds of spouses, then the key to understanding marriage and divorce lies not in the detailed dynamics of dating and household life but rather in the larger barriers that shape "pools" of partners likely to come together—barriers like college attendance, for example. Moreover, we can put the issue of partner choice in motion, for as everyone knows, the number of plausible candidates available in the market declines rapidly at certain stages in the life course—for example, at the end of one's college or graduate school years. This makes us think about another counterfactual: how would people go about finding and sampling partners if there were no such thing as college? (That is, do colleges have the latent function of facilitating the marriage market?) Of course, there is a natural experiment of sorts for that proposition, since much of the population doesn't go to college. (And note that that portion of the population tends to marry earlier!)

Thus, starting with a simple counterfactual spins us out, via a number of other heuristic leaps, into a wide variety of interesting hypotheses about marriage and marriage patterns. This is the utility of counterfactual analysis. It drives us to problematize the obvious and suggests dozens of new ways in which to think.

COUNTERFACTUALS BRING US to the end of this survey of general heuristic gambits. This chapter and the preceding one have discussed a wide variety of ways of producing new ideas. I should underscore—as I have before and will again—that these heuristics should not be reified. They are not about the true and the untrue but about finding new ideas. They should be taken as aids to reflection, not as fixed things.

They are also very powerful. Although many of these examples have involved more than one heuristic move, you should use them one at a time and carefully work out the results of each one. Otherwise, they can get you into deep water very quickly.

These general heuristics are not the final or even the most powerful set of heuristic tools for social science. That honor goes to the fractal heuristics founded on the basic debates of Chapter Two. I now turn to them.

Chapter Six
FRACTAL HEURISTICS

WE HAVE SO FAR SEEN three general types of heuristics. The simplest are additive rules for creating minor variations in ideas. The second are lists of generic topics and common notions that we can use as stimuli to point us in new directions. The third—the general heuristics of Chapters Four and Five— are more self-conscious devices for producing new ideas by manipulating arguments, descriptions, and narratives in particular ways.

In this chapter, I take up a fourth type of heuristic, one that arises in the "great debates" of the social sciences that I discussed in Chapter Two. It makes use of a particular quality of these debates, one that I noted briefly at the end of that chapter: their fractal nature. A fractal is simply something that

looks the same no matter how close we get to it. A famous fractal is the woodland fern, each of whose fronds is a little fern
made of leaves that are actually little ferns made up of tinier
ferns, and so on.

The great debates I discussed in Chapter Two are fractals in
the sense that they seem to be important debates no matter
what the level of investigation at which we take them up. Take
the famous opposition of realists and constructionists. Realists
think social reality is a real thing, fixed and repeatable. Constructionists don't. Constructionists think the actors and meanings of social life are made up as we go along, by playing with
past repertoires. Realists don't.

Now most sociologists have a pretty clear idea of who the
realists are and who the constructionists are. Survey analysts are
usually thought to be realists and historical sociologists to be
constructionists. Stratification scholars are usually realists; sociologists of science are constructionists—and so on. But suppose
we take some sociologists of science and isolate them somehow.
Sure enough, they will start to argue internally over precisely
this issue of realism and constructionism. Some will argue that
science is a given type of knowledge produced by a certain kind
of social structure; the big issue is how that knowledge is
shaped by larger social structures. Others will argue that you
cannot understand what science itself is until you understand
the actual flow of the daily language that scientists use to build
the scientific knowledge that gets rationalized in textbooks.
That is, the two groups will fall into violent debates over
precisely the issue of realism versus constructionism even
though the rest of the discipline regards them all as strong constructionists. (This is, in fact, exactly what happened in the

sociology of science in the 1980s, when the field had a kind of "I think more things are socially constructed than you do" contest that ended up with the whole field pretending, somewhat nervously, that it didn't believe in the reality of anything at all.)

To take an example on the other side of the discipline, the sociology of crime was for a long time one of the strong realist fields in sociology. Crime statistics have a long history in American public life, and few events seemed more obviously real than an arrest. But in the 1950s, there emerged within this highly realist literature a constructionist critique. This "labeling theory" argued that there was something more to becoming a criminal than simply doing the act; you had to get caught, detained, held, charged, convicted, and sentenced. Many people slipped away at each step along the way, yet only at the end did you really become a labeled "criminal." The labelers insisted that the long-observed inverse correlation between social status and criminality happened because lower-class offenders were more likely to make it through the long process that leads from act to conviction. Criminality was not a simple, real fact but a complex, constructed one.

Meanwhile, there was also a similar but smaller debate within the *purely realist* group of criminologists. These realists were in an uproar because of the unreliability of arrest statistics. Chicago's crime rate rose 83 percent in one year (1962), and everyone knew that reality had not changed but reporting procedures had. So a vociferous group argued that arrest statistics were arbitrarily constructed and crime should be measured by surveys of victims, not by counts of offenders. And in setting up the victimization surveys, dozens of realist/constructionist questions were asked: Is a series of harassing acts one event or many? Do closed-form survey questions necessarily coerce respondents to follow a certain pattern? When is a question to be considered "suggestive"? These were all the same debates that the sociologists of science were to have in the 1980s, but they were located in a community that the discipline widely regarded as realist.

As this example shows, the central social scientific debates of Chapter Two are fractal in nature. No matter how large or how small the community of social scientists we consider, most of these issues will be debated within it, even if we think that the community already represents one extreme or the other on the issue. By itself, that is just a curious fact. But this curious fact means that we can use the basic debates as heuristic tools. Wherever we find ourselves with respect to the complex arrangement of forms of knowledge that is social science, we can always use these fractal heuristics to produce new questions and new problems.

A simple example of this comes from the literature on anxiety and stress. How are we to explain stress? Who suffers most? What can stop it or mediate it? The literature investigating these questions from the 1960s through the 1980s was strongly positivist. But what is most noticeable to an outsider reading the stress literature is that whenever the positivist researchers came up against a blank wall, they would develop *narratives* and *reinterpretations* of data that would open new research vistas for them. Thus, the original literature looked only at the correlation between stressors (unusual events) and distress (unhappiness). When those correlations proved to be weak, researchers started to think about "coping," defined as a mediating phenomenon on the path (that is, in the narrative) from stressors to distress. Differences in coping skills and resources would account for the weak simple correlation between stressors and distress: better copers would suffer less from a given number of stressors than weaker copers would. When these coping variables proved weak in their turn, analysts started asking even more subtle interpretive questions, such as "[a]t what point does heavy drinking change from a coping strategy into a symptom?" (Kessler, Price, and Wortman 1985:552). Now the answer to this last question has been the subject of numerous famous novels (for example, Fitzgerald's *The Beautiful and Damned*) and films (for example, *The Days of Wine and Roses*), which show well that there is nothing like an objective answer to it. But just thinking about it gave the stress positivists something new to do. They weren't stuck any longer in their cul-de-sac with the lousy correlations. They had new questions to investigate.

That is what I mean when I say that the main importance of the fractal debates may not be as organizing principles of the disciplines, but rather as heuristics for the disciplines. Indeed, I might even propose that the great debates had their *first* existence as heuristics and became general, organizing principles for how we view whole disciplines and methods only because so many kinds of people, believing so many substantive things, used them as heuristics. On this argument, it is their widespread use as heuristics that leads theorists of various disciplines to assemble all the locally different uses into what appear to be grand organizing debates. Here I'm just pulling one of my own heuristic tricks: reverse the direction of causation, and see if your argument is still credible! I'm not sure whether this argument holds—and this is not the place to evaluate it—but it's an interesting possibility in the historical sociology of social science.

In summary, the great central debates of social science are themselves widely (if implicitly) used in a heuristic mode to open up new questions and possibilities. In this guise, they are as common a heuristic as any of the others I have examined. Like other heuristics, they can be greatly overused. And like other heuristics, they should not be taken to be the one, true nature of things. (That has been the problem with treating them as great debates.) But treated well, they will be a useful part of your heuristic armamentarium, good anywhere anytime.

I shall organize this chapter according to the nine basic debates discussed in Chapter Two. For each debate, I shall give a few examples, trying to show how each one can be used no matter what the method, no matter what the current definitions of the research. I do not give examples for both choices for each of my five methodological traditions. That would be 90 examples (2 choices × 5 methods × 9 debates), and you don't want to read them all any more than I want to go looking for them all. But I shall try to offer enough possibilities to give you a sense of the richness of fractal heuristics. And I shall emphasize moves that went against the grain: deep interpretivists who turn positivist, emergentists who try out individualism, and so on. As before, I have tried to select papers that have had a strong influence on subsequent social science, although in some cases, I've been seduced by favorite recent work. I apologize in advance for the almost bewildering diversity of the examples, but that is part of the point; fractal heuristics are used throughout the social sciences in a bewildering variety of ways.

I. POSITIVISM AND INTERPRETIVISM

The first of the fractal debates is between positivism and interpretivism, between thinking you can and should measure social
reality formally and thinking you can't and shouldn't. In fact,
it is easy to find examples of positivist and interpretive moves
in nearly any methodological tradition. The two are engaged in
an incessant dialogue. So in ethnography, sometimes our impulse is to count things (as William F. Whyte counted bowling
scores in *Street Corner Society*), and sometimes our impulse is to
delve into even more interpretive detail (as Mitchell Duneier
does in discussing police busts in *Sidewalk*). In SCA-type analysis, the moves toward positivism are too numerous to count,
but there are equally as many moves the other way, as I just
noted in my discussion of the stress literature.

A particularly elegant example of an interpretivist move in
positivist work is Richard Berk and Sarah Fenstermaker Berk's
influential article on models for the household division of labor
(1978). Berk and Berk are attempting to evaluate the "new"
home economics, with its theory of the household as a production system. They employ an extremely elaborate positivist design: a two-stage least squares operationalization of a structural
equation model for a data set on the allocation of household
tasks. But the article ends up in an interpretive discussion
about the definition of "sharing" and "substitution" in household tasks. Noting the complex differences between husbands' and wives' effects on the household division of labor
(changes in which tasks the wife does affect which tasks the
husband does but not vice versa), the authors point out that husbands tend to participate jointly with other family members in

production, and they provide quotations from respondents illustrating three different models for this "sharing": "moral support," "assistance," and "supervised help." These definitions of sharing have different implications for the substitution of the husbands' effort for the wives' effort and hence for the project of analyzing the family as a production system. Berk and Berk leave the reader wondering about the question of the exact trade-off between husbands' and wives' housework. In short, after all the rules are followed and all the regressions are run, the way out of a quantitative dilemma takes the form of reinterpreting a variable by anchoring it in a more complicated story with more ambiguous meanings. Thus, a positivist blind alley is escaped via an interpretive move.

It is equally important to note moves toward positivism in a place like historical analysis, where we least expect it. One example is the paper by V. O. Key on critical elections (1955), one of the single most influential papers in political science in the twentieth century. Key's paper removes elections from the one-by-one tell-a-story approach that had been common before his time. By analyzing detailed counts of votes in particular constituencies over many national elections in a row, he showed that in certain elections there were sudden realignments that then persisted for three or four elections thereafter. Key's move might be seen as a form of temporal lumping; his argument was that the "event" of realignment was often bigger and more enduring than it seemed. But it is important to see that Key made his claim stand by taking a distinctly positivist turn in a literature that was until then given mostly to historical, discursive analysis. It was by getting analytic that Key made his mark.

A similar, much more recent move occurs in John Mohr's brilliant analysis of images of poverty in nineteenth-century New York (Mohr and Duquenne 1997). Mohr sought to uncover New Yorkers' images and concepts of poor and needy people. Rather than follow the normal strategy of critical analysis of texts about poverty, he fed the official descriptions of clienteles from dozens of New York social service agencies into a computer. He then analyzed these official descriptions by saying that two types of needy people were "close," in the eyes of New Yorkers, if they appeared in the same descriptions together. Once he had calculated the "closeness" of all possible pairs of types, he could use clustering and scaling methods that turn such "distance" data into clusters and pictures. As a result, he produced an astoundingly comprehensive picture of poverty as it was envisioned by the very agencies that dealt with it. The move was a radically positivist one, but it revealed aspects of nineteenth-century theories of poverty that had never yet been conceived.

In short, we find that the positivist/interpretivist choice can be made by any kind of analyst at any point. Often, as in the cases mentioned here, the moves have their most decisive effect when they go against the expected direction. We don't expect an interpretive move in SCA, and we don't expect positivist moves in historical and cultural analysis. Therefore, the results of such moves seem all the more dazzling. In fact, either move is possible in any method at any point.

And at any level! One can easily envision moving on to the next level of detail and making either move with respect to any of these examples. Take critical elections. It is clear that one could get far more positivist than Key in evaluating the question of whether critical elections really do exist, and indeed there is a large literature since Key that has done just that. One can also imagine making the move to counting election results and to examining longer runs of elections, as Key did, but then insisting on a more interpretive form of analysis of the results. Key's own rendition of the phenomenon, in the original paper, is completely demographic. He simply identifies the phenomenon in the voting patterns but makes no attempt to interpret it. Was it a result of new party ideologies? of new party organization? of legal changes in registration? Was it a downstream result of the changed immigration laws of 1924? of a new voting coalition in subgroups? of a change of heart by some major subgroup? The possibilities are many and immediately encourage a large interpretive, historical literature, which did in fact emerge to try to explain the phenomenon Key had uncovered.

In short, not only is the pairing of positivist with interpretivist a heuristic pairing useful across all methods, but it also applies at any level in those methods. This pairing is truly a fractal heuristic. If your current thinking is blocked, one way to move ahead is to use it to sidestep the blockage and open up new research problems and opportunities.

II. ANALYSIS AND NARRATION

Like positivism and interpretivism, the pairing of analysis and narration is used throughout social science as a fractal heuristic. Sometimes we need to follow a story through as a story, sometimes we need to break it into bits and compare the bits, but no matter what the method or the level, the switch between narration and analysis is always available and often used.

In the first instance, this switch can be seen as simply the narrative heuristic of freezing or setting in motion, discussed in the preceding chapter. For example, in one of the most influential theoretical papers of gender literature, Candace West and Don Zimmerman argued that "gender is not a set of traits, nor a variable, nor a role, but the product of social doings of some sort" (1987:129). That is, gender is a performance, a process of making certain gestures and invoking certain symbols in certain contexts with the intent of pointing to oneself as gendered. The insistence that gender is not a fixed thing but an ongoing performance challenges gender research whatever the method it employs. In ethnography, it means forgetting about preexisting gender roles and watching how people mark gender distinctions over time. In SCA analysis like the Berk and Berk paper just mentioned, it means investigating trade-offs in housework over time rather than assuming that there are stable contributions of men and women. And so on.

But the analysis/narration heuristic move is often not just a matter of setting in motion or stopping but can be a specific move with respect to a particular current method. In ethnography, for example, the strong drift of the last twenty years has been toward much more narrative, temporal approaches. The new ethnography embeds its local events in larger narratives of culture contact (as in the work of Marshall Sahlins on Captain Cook in Hawaii [1985]), developing capitalism (as in the work of Michael Burawoy on de-skilling in American factories [1979]), globalization (as in Janet Salaff's work on young girls in Hong Kong factories [1981]), or some other large-scale historical process. Even in anthropological linguistics, which relies far more on technical and analytic machinery than the rest of anthropology, the move toward more narrative methods has been marked. Indeed, the drift to narration is so strong that ethnography is ripe for an antihistorical move—perhaps based on an ahistorical theory like rational choice, perhaps based on a renewed insistence on local ethnographic validity.

The constant tug of war between narrative and analytic moves is even more evident if we consider not a particular methodological tradition but a general field of research. Studies of social class in modern societies are a good example. The great classic of mid-twentieth-century social-class studies was W. Lloyd Warner's immense "Yankee City" study of Newburyport, Massachusetts, a kind of industrial-strength ethnography done by dozens of workers who talked to hundreds of people and evaluated their class status based on their language, furniture, place of residence, and many other things (Warner et al. 1963). The social-class concept Warner used in this work was highly analytic and static (Warner, Meeker, and Eells 1949). Not surprisingly, it was widely attacked by historians. While some of the attacks were, predictably, based on the simple "putting into motion" heuristic (that is, "Warner got it wrong because he took a snapshot when he should have watched the movie"), the most damaging was Stephan Thernstrom's highly analytic study *Poverty and Progress*. Thernstrom traced individuals through manuscript census records, counted noses, and showed that there was far more class mobility than Warner had suspected.

From our point of view, Thernstrom made a narrative move in that he looked at the life histories of individuals rather than simply talking to all of the residents of Newburyport at one point. He made it in a very analytic way, however, in that he did not interview people or seek detailed histories of individuals, but rather reduced their lives to coded sequences of the class statuses they successively held over time. This narrative move with an analytic accent contrasts strongly with the contemporary move by Blau and Duncan's already discussed *American Occupational Structure*. These students of mobility—and indeed the whole tradition they stood in—conceived of the "narrative" of mobility as a jump from the static class status of a father to the static class status of a son. The move was analytic at nearly all levels, assuming away most of the lifetime change in the father's class standing, most of the change in the prestige structure of occupations, and (as we have seen in an earlier chapter) all of the cross-individual variation in the "narrative" pattern of causes. All of this in order to make dramatic analytic comparisons.

To make so many analytic moves—moves away from narration—sounds worrisome, of course, but it is important to realize that a literature has to make such choices in order to move ahead. The sociological-mobility literature deliberately assumed away certain parts of the history in order to get at others. For example, the enormously influential paper of Robert Hodge, Paul Siegel, and Peter Rossi on the "history" of occupational prestige in the United States establishes that the occupational prestige ratings are stable over time (1966), a crucial element in the structural view taken by the Blau and Duncan book and most later sociological study of mobility. But the Hodge, Siegel, and Rossi paper accomplished this by assuming that there were no changes in the nature of occupations themselves between 1925 and 1963. That assumption was necessary, of course, if we were to think that people were rating the prestige of the same things throughout the period. But in fact, the identities of occupations like secretary and bookkeeper changed almost completely in that period. Ignoring that change—at least for a while—was the price that had to be paid. Only by assuming away some parts of a narrative can you open other parts to analysis.

Before leaving the fractal heuristic of analysis/narration, we should consider some examples of studies that move with the grain rather than against it, studies that are already highly analytic but make a decisive move to become even more so or studies that are already narrative but make further narrative moves. The reader should not think that against the grain is the only possibility.

An example of narrative analysis that deepens itself by moving to an even more complex narrative level is Goran Therborn's influential paper on "The Rule of Capital and the Rise of Democracy." Therborn's paper considers one of the classic narrative problems—the rise of democracy—by comparing (in capsule form) the histories of two dozen modern democracies. His argument starts where Barrington Moore's *Social Origins of Dictatorship and Democracy* leaves off, with the notion that the rise of democracy is a complex and contingent process, not the result of a single variable or constellation of variables, as it appeared to be in the much more analytic work of Seymour Martin Lipset and others. But Therborn insists that prior narrative analyses have left out another narrative essentially related to that of democratization: participation in or threat of foreign war. He makes a strong case that war or its threat was central in forcing bourgeois states to spread access to power and authority more broadly throughout their populations. He thus took what was already a comparison of complex historical narratives and made them even more complex. (Note that his move was not simply to introduce a single variable of war but rather to look at the different roles different wars played in each of the historical trajectories he examined.)

An even more striking example (but in the other direction) is John Muth's "Rational Expectations and the Theory of Price Movements," a paper that lay unnoticed for a decade, until Robert Lucas and others fashioned from its kernel a theory that transformed our view of government intervention in the economy. Muth, an economist, makes a strongly analytic move in a tradition of research that is already highly analytic; not only are economic actors "rational maximizers" at the first level, he says, but they in fact act the way *economists* would. The paper starts with a purely formal analysis of an economy in which producers are predicting the prices they will be able to get for their goods in future time intervals. It specifically attacks Herbert Simon's hypothesis of "bounded rationality" (discussed in Chapter Four; see Simon 1982):

> It is sometimes argued that the assumption of rationality in economics leads to theories inconsistent with, or inadequate to explain, observed phenomena, especially changes over time. . . . Our hypothesis is based on exactly the opposite point of view: that dynamic economic models do not assume *enough* rationality. (Muth 1961:316; emphasis added)

Muth's argument is essentially that if there *were* a substantial and predictable difference between firms' expectations and the behavior of the market, someone would have been able to create a firm or a speculation taking advantage of it. On the general economic assumption that people are rational, someone would therefore have done that (if it were possible), and therefore we are safe in assuming that prices as they currently exist reveal all such predictions about the future, including secret speculative ones. For if secret speculative reward exists, then someone has taken advantage of it and hence removed the possibility from the market.[1] Muth's argument was later used to attack Keynesian management of the economy. Since government fiscal policy was a matter of public record, it was argued, speculators would take advantage of any difference between government-supported prices and "real market" prices, in the process canceling the effects of government intervention.

Our interest here is less in the policy implications of Muth's celebrated article than in its seemingly extremist insistence that an already absolutely analytic literature become even more analytic. Effectively, the Muth paper assumed that at least at the level of expectations, firms (as a group) were as good at predicting the future as were economists. As Muth himself pointed out, this was quite close to "stating that the marginal revenue product of economics is zero" (1961:316). Not only were economists analytic, but they also might as well assume that the firms they studied were as analytic as they. This extraordinary assumption produced two or three decades of exciting research before the rational-expectations hypothesis was finally deserted for newer, more exciting ideas.

Thus the analysis/narration debate also functions as a fractal distinction. We should note, however, that the order in which one takes narrative or analytic turns makes a big difference. Taking a narrative turn after an analytic one does not get you to the same place as taking an analytic turn after a narrative one.

A good illustration of this comes from the story of my own borrowing of optimal-matching methods from biology, mentioned in Chapter Four. I did this borrowing because I had decided that it was important to think about the full sequences of people's careers rather than just each separate instance of employment and occupation. That is, I made a narrative turn first, toward treating the full sequence of someone's work life as important. My next turn was analytic; I realized that I could compare careers by employing the sequencing-comparison algorithms that were used to compare strands of DNA. The algorithms would create "distances" between careers, and I could then classify them, using the usual array of pattern search methods.

By comparison, if when we study workers, we make the analytic turn first, we inevitably think of individual episodes of particular workers' being employed to do particular things at a given moment. This in turn leads to thinking in terms of labor markets, where these worker-job units are transacted. If we then make a narrative move and start to ask about the changing nature of some particular labor market, we are seeing a different set of things than are visible using the methods I developed. We don't have a continuous set of people but rather a continuous set of transactions. The questions of interest aren't patterns in people's careers but rather the historical developments of a general labor market: changes in likelihood of hiring, changes in hiring firms, changes in types of individuals hired, and so on.

Note that both sets of questions are interesting. It is not that one set is the right set and one the wrong. Rather, they're both interesting and important questions, but for different reasons to different people with respect to different theories. The example shows that the order in which you invoke fractal heuristics has a big impact on where you end up.

III. Behaviorism and Culturalism

With the heuristic involving behaviorism and culturalism, we move away from debates about forms of analysis to the heuristics drawing on differences in how we think about the ontology of social life—the elements and processes that we imagine make up the world. In this first case, the issue is whether we focus on social structure or on culture, on observable behavior or on meaning.

One of the best examples of this heuristic I have already given: Howard Becker's magnificent paper on marijuana use. I used this as an example of making a reversal in Chapter Four. The reversal Becker made involved just this heuristic. Rather than assuming that attitudes precede behavior, as is more or less standard, Becker argued that behavior produces attitudes. He was playing with our sense of the relation between behavior and meaning.

A useful way to see the fractal character of this contrast is to look at two influential papers, both in a single methodological tradition (SCA), one of which takes a behaviorist turn and one a cultural turn. We normally think of the SCA tradition of methods as largely behaviorist, unconcerned with the meanings of things, but even within that framework it is possible to move in either direction. As it happens, both of these papers consider the application of economic ideas to family life. In one that application is part of the hypothesis, while in the other it is something to be explained.

First, a move toward behavior. George Farkas's "Education, Wage Rates, and the Division of Labor between Husband and Wife" was one of the first papers to look directly at the family-division-of-labor question with strong modern data. Not surprisingly, it has been very influential. It is a model of social science, with excellent data and effective analysis and, perhaps more important, with clear alternative hypotheses to which the author gives equal attention. Farkas aims to test three basic theories about the household division of labor: the economist's "wage rate" view that couples seek to maximize total household utility and hence adjust their division of labor to the relative ability of husband and wife to make money outside the household; the "subcultural" theory that middle- and upper-class husbands and wives are more likely to accept women's work outside the home; and the "relative resources" argument that relative differences in education (*not* available wages outside the home) drive the division of labor.

What is behaviorist about the paper is its insistence that we examine not attitudes about the household division of labor but actual performance. Hence, the dependent variables are the wife's annual work outside the home and the husband's reported hours of housework. Most earlier work on households was based on ethnographic or interview-based research that gave less attention to behavior than to attitudes. Indeed, it was clear from the earlier research that those attitudes took the form implied in the relative resources and subcultural hypotheses. What was not known was whether behavior did as well. Did upper- and middle-class households just talk a good line, or did they live it? It was easy to suspect that couples might talk a more egalitarian line than they actually lived. As it happened, Farkas found that the relative-resources (educational differences) theory did badly, subculture (class differences) did best, but the wage-rate (ecological) theory could not be ruled out. As often happens, the big results were surprises; that the presence of children played a central role in determining the division of labor, and that division of labor changed radically over a family's life cycle.

For us, the important matter here is that by insisting on predicting behavior, not attitudes, Farkas made a distinctly behaviorist move within a tradition generally regarded as already quite behaviorist. It was a matter of doing what we already do, but doing it better. We can see the contrasting move—which is more surprising—in Ron Lesthaeghe's widely cited "Century of Demographic and Cultural Change in Western Europe." Lesthaeghe's paper advances our understanding of changes in demographic behavior, but it does so by moving toward culture.

There are two heuristic moves involved in the paper. The first is locating demographic change within something larger. This move of lumping things together is one of the descriptive heuristics of Chapter Five. An important consequence of Lesthaeghe's choice of the lumping heuristic is that he employs a quantitative technique aimed specifically at lumping: factor analysis. As opposed to SCA's much more common regression techniques, which are designed to separate the effects of different variables, factor analysis specifically asks whether certain variables cannot be lumped together as part of larger phenomena. (It is important to realize that once one starts looking, there are formal, mathematical methods for many heuristic moves. Statistical and mathematical techniques reach far more broadly than a glance at the journals—or a course on sociological statistics—might make you think.)

For our purposes, Lesthaeghe's paper is less interesting for its lumping than for its move toward culture. This is clear from the opening sentences:

> A fertility decline is in essence part of a broader emancipation process. More specifically, the demographic regulatory mechanisms, upheld by the accompanying communal or family authority and exchange patterns, give way to the principle of freedom of choice, thereby allowing an extension of the domain of economic rationality to the phenomenon of reproduction. . . . The purpose of this exercise is to explore the extent to which current changes in fertility and nuptiality can be viewed as manifestations of a cultural dimension that had already emerged at the time of the demographic transition in Europe. (Lesthaeghe 1983:411)

In making this move, Lesthaeghe moved very much against the grain of demography as a social science. Demography is in many ways one of the most behaviorist of the social sciences. Its central variables are rates of four unmistakably explicit behaviors: birth, marriage, death, and migration. The apparatus of life-table analysis, through which rates of these four behaviors can produce estimates of populations' age and marriage structures, is one of the glories of formal social science. Yet Lesthaeghe's whole enterprise in this influential article is to make us see demographic change as a part of a cultural shift, not a behavioral one. And he manages to use quantitative techniques to do it!

We see, then, that within a particular tradition of methods that is widely understood as strongly behaviorist, it is still possible to move in either direction. Farkas's move is strongly toward behavior that can be measured. Lesthaeghe's is toward a cultural construct (the rise of individualism) that can be "measured" only as an implicit commonality among existing sets of measured variables. Once again, we see that a commitment at one level to one or the other side of a fractal heuristic does not translate into a commitment at the next level. All roads are always open.

IV. INDIVIDUALISM AND EMERGENTISM

The debate over individuals and emergents has been one of the most enduring in social science. Methodological individualists are forever insisting that only individuals are real. Yet most of us are closet emergentists with working beliefs in social groups and forces. Philosophically, emergentism has found itself the embattled position. Every reader of Durkheim's *Suicide* knows that the author spends many (probably too many) pages defending his emergentist views and attacking individualism.

Yet this pairing, too, can be a fractal heuristic. Emergentist literatures invoke individualist theories and vice versa. One can see this in any methods tradition. In ethnography, for example, the dominant tradition is ethnography of groups, from Malinowski onward. Yet there is an equally old tradition of individual study or life history, beginning with W. I. Thomas and Florian Znaniecki's five-volume series on *The Polish Peasant in*

Europe and America, which was largely built on life histories and life-history documents. The historical turn of anthropology has brought a renewal of such a focus on individuals, as in Sahlins's work on Captain Cook in the Hawaiian Islands. Historical analysis has of course seesawed for many decades between "great man" biographical history and corporate history. Within particular historical works, the two levels of analysis are often completely intertwined.

Again, a good way to see this fractal duality in action is to discuss contrasting papers within one major method tradition, in this case, formalism. Among the most famous books in social science over the last half century is *The Logic of Collective Action* by Mancur Olson, Jr. Olson's basic aim is to show why people join groups and participate in group activities; he starts from a resolutely individualist premise: he wants to question the notion that people join groups because of the benefits they get from them. He notes that groups often provide benefits for all their members, whether the members contribute or not. When it comes to these collective goods, as they are called, those who can get away with it have every incentive to take them without contributing anything. (Those who do so are the "free riders." Olson's was the analysis that popularized the concept—but not the term—of "free riding.") But if this is the case, how can we explain why groups that provide collective goods ever exist? Olson's answer to this question was ingenious, invoking what he called selective incentives—various ways the group has of targeting those who contribute (giving them positive rewards) and those who don't (giving them punishments). Of course, there were further problems (who was to pay for the system of selective incentives? and so on), but the book ignited a debate on the nature of collective action that continues to this day. All of this was argued in the classic formal style of economics, using fairly simple representations of supply, demand, contribution, and so on. And all of it started in the traditional manner, with isolated individuals.

At the same time Olson was writing, the sociologist Harrison White was moving in precisely the other direction. White employed similarly formal methods to ask nearly the reverse question: not how is it that individuals with similar interests get together in groups but rather should we define individuals as similar when they are located in similar positions in all of their social groups? For Olson, similarity of individual interests came first, and location in groups (with the aim of collaborating on producing collective goods) came second. For White, it was exactly the other way around. Location in groups came first, and we could understand people as being similar (in interests or in anything else) if their patterns of social location were similar.

François Lorrain and Harrison White's "Structural Equivalence of Individuals in Social Networks" starts not from the notion that there are individuals and groups but, rather, from the notion that there are individuals and types of relations between them. As is often the case with such original papers, many levels of complexity were included in this exposition that have since been forgotten. But hidden in the complexity and couched in the impenetrable mathematics of category theory was a concept that would revolutionize the study of networks: the concept of structural equivalence. Loosely speaking, structurally equivalent actors are defined as those actors all of whose network ties are the same:

In other words, a is structurally equivalent to b if a relates to
every object x of C in exactly the same ways as b does. From
the point of view of the logic of the structure, then, a and b
are absolutely equivalent, they are substitutable. Indeed, in
such a case there is no reason not to identify a and b. (Lorrain
and White 1971:63)

White and his collaborators and followers would elaborate the
concept of structural equivalence, making it into a comprehensive model for understanding roles and social structures.
Similarity became network similarity. Relations come first; individuals second.

Once again, then, we see that moves toward individual conceptions or emergent ones are possible despite the usual association of formalization with methodological individualism. The
history of network analysis is extremely instructive in this regard. The "individualist" network analysts (those opposed to
White—James Coleman, for example) conceived of networks
largely in terms of cliques and measured "centrality" in networks, whereas the emergentists like White (usually called
structuralists in this literature) focused on structural equivalence. The structuralist Ronald Burt wrote a widely cited paper
in which he tested the two against each other (1983). Not surprisingly given Burt's allegiance, structural equivalence won.
But the individualists went merrily on and eventually developed the notion that having a lot of network ties was a kind of
resource for individuals. Baptised by Pierre Bourdieu and James
Coleman with the name social capital, this notion has become
one of the great growth concepts of the 1990s, now virtually a
standard variable in traditional SCA-type analyses of field after

field. Meanwhile, the structuralists have pared down the elaborate logic of multiple types of relations that drove White's original work and are developing "network" concepts of markets that invoke many of the classical incentive theories of traditional microeconomics. Peter Abell wrote about "games in networks" (1990), bringing together the structural concept of networks and the relatively individualistic concepts of game theory.

So this fractal heuristic, too, is steadily taking new turns within the old turns, and so on. Just as it drives the research frontier, so also is it available for us in more routine social science. Making a move toward individualism or emergentism is always available as a means of rethinking a problem or finding a new line of investigation.

V. REALISM AND CONSTRUCTIONISM

The interplay of realism and constructionism is probably the most familiar of these debates. We have spent the last thirty years hearing the phrase "social construction" applied to nearly everything in the social world: race, gender, class, nationality, ethnicity, aesthetic judgment, scientific knowledge—whatever.

Because of this huge amount of material, there is relatively little need to illustrate constructionist moves. Readers are no doubt already familiar with them. But there are some particularly interesting versions of constructionism, and it is useful to look at those. Among the most exciting, because they have such a big potential impact on social science research, are the analyses of social statistics showing that our very census figures embody dozens of arbitrary and often deliberately questionable coding decisions. Writers like Alain Desrosières, Simon Szreter, and Margo Anderson have shown, for example, that the occupational statistics we use to measure achievement were quite arbitrarily developed and, more important, that they change arbitrarily from census to census.[2] Where do we count family workers—wives and husbands and cousins and uncles who help out occasionally in their relatives' businesses? What do we do with the vast penumbra of "invisible work"—casual work for cash in the informal economy of cleaning, child care, lawn mowing, and so on? What do we make of illegal labor—paid work in the drug industry, for example? What do we do when the name of an occupation doesn't change but its status and its typical employees do, as happened to the position of secretary in the early years of the twentieth century?

One has only to pose these questions to realize that what seemed to be methodological problems are all the openings of major research traditions. Figuring out how our labels for occupations came into existence and how loosely the labels are related to the realities underneath will tell us extremely important things about the labor market. Understanding the creation of the census category of housewife tells us more about how work was structured in the nineteenth century than could a dozen studies treating the census categories as unproblematic.

It is also true that once you make the first constructionist move—say, you dig up all the types of jobs that got mixed into and out of the category of bookkeeper—you then face the important *realist* task of assembling an image of what that constructed world looks like as a "constructedly" real one. In the case of bookkeepers, you have to go on to generate a firm "historical" series of occupational numbers. The constructionist move is often a debunking move and all too often stops there.

When you make a constructionist move, always go on to make a realist turn. Once you've opened things up with constructionism, it is time to figure out the real consequences of that construction.

Still, one wonders whether the heuristic can first move the other way, against constructionism. Are there papers that deliberately undercut social construction, papers that push us toward realism? One is Daniel Chambliss's classic "Mundanity of Excellence." Chambliss spent five years studying competitive swimming. He coached from the local to the national levels, interviewed dozens of swimmers, and traveled with the best teams in the country. His core research problem was to discover the nature of "talent" and "excellence" in swimming. His central conclusion was that talent was a complete fabrication, a meaningless construction designed to cover and romanticize what he called "the mundanity of excellence":

> Superb performance is really a confluence of dozens of small skills or activities, each one learned or stumbled upon, which have been carefully drilled into habit and then are fitted together in a synthesized whole. There is nothing extraordinary or superhuman in any one of those actions: only the fact that they are done consistently and correctly, and all together, produced excellence. (Chambliss 1989:81)

Great champions are people who work on the details and make sure they do all of them right all of the time. Their motivations were also "mundane." They didn't aim to win the Olympics as much as to polish up their backstroke next week, improve their sleep habits over the next month, and eat more carefully. In short, their goals were nearby, not far off. Indeed, Chambliss argued, the great champions try to turn the big meets into mundane occasions by making every single day a big meet, winning every single race in practice. The big ones then meant nothing more than the others.

Chambliss's move is to argue that a particular social construction (talent) is simply a label for the success that it supposedly explains. It does not refer to anything at all. Differences in small routine practices explain success in swimming. We can see this move as a behaviorist one, because of the insistence on looking at small practices. But the opposite of a behaviorist move would be a culturalist one, and talent (as opposed to the routine behaviors of doing a turn better or sleeping well) is not so much a cultural or subjective thing as it is a simple reification, an unreality. (So this move could have been stimulated by one of my commonplace lists.) Believing in talent means believing that there must be some one thing that makes for consistent success in swimming and that, although we don't know exactly what it is, we should give it a single name: talent. It is a rather simple social construction that gets in the way of our understanding the real sources of consistent excellence in swimming.

Not surprisingly, Chambliss's piece drew fire from more strongly constructionist writers. Tia DeNora chided him for not recognizing that in many other fields (Chambliss had offered tentative generalizations) even the standards of winning were negotiated between performers and audiences (for example, in the arts). Chambliss's argument, she felt, "cultivated an inappropriately meritocratic imagery of excellence and ranking" (1992:102). That is, she attacked Chambliss for treating winning itself not as socially constructed but as real. Chambliss admitted, in response, that it was quite arbitrary (and hence socially constructed) that we rated swimmers by their times instead of their beauty (the way we rate divers) or the technical precision of their strokes. But once that decision is made, "we still can define excellence provisionally as consistent superiority in meeting that standard" (1992:105). In the dictum of W. I. Thomas, "[I]f men define situations as real, they are real in their consequences" (Thomas and Thomas 1928:572).

Chambliss's paper and the debate it inspired show well the fluid power of the heuristic that flows from the realist/constructionist debate. Everyone involved in the debate was identified, at least by the majority of the discipline, with methods and subfields that are considered to be overwhelmingly committed to constructionism. But even within this small and fairly consistent group of scholars, Chambliss's realist turn produced an extraordinarily heated debate.

The realist/constructionist debate and the heuristic that flows from it are probably the most familiar of the debate heuristics I discuss. It is essential to realize that heuristic use of such a debate does not aim at debunking or demolishing—two common reasons for making constructionist and realist moves, respectively. The idea of heuristics is to open up new topics, to find new things. To do that, sometimes we need to invoke constructionism, as have the students of occupational prestige. Sometimes we need a little realism, such as we are given by Chambliss. In both cases—indeed, with all of the heuristics discussed here—the idea is to open things up. Once they are open, the excitement lies in following new leads, not trashing our opponents.

VI. CONTEXTUALISM AND NONCONTEXTUALISM

The fractal debate over invoking or ignoring contexts is the last of the debates arising from issues of social ontology. The issue here is which way one ought to move to improve and deepen one's knowledge of a problem. The contextual strategy is to look beyond our immediate concern to see how it is embedded in the larger social world. The noncontextualizing strategy is to mark our problem off and generalize it by finding comparable units or problems elsewhere.

In the recent history of the social sciences, noncontextualizing is the program of most of the "scientizers." Contextualizing has most often been the program of those resisting scientization. But when one looks at research, it is clear that the moves of recognizing the context or of explicitly choosing to ignore an important context occur throughout social science heuristics. As before, I shall emphasize moves against the grain, since they illustrate the power of such a heuristic particularly well.

I begin with the move of contextualizing. SCA analyses generally avoid this. For example, throughout this book I have presented examples from the large literature on stratification, most of them looking at individual achievement in terms of the particular attributes of individuals. This is a noncontextualizing strategy. The parameters measuring the effects of education or occupation or father's occupation on a respondent's current income or achievement are estimated on the assumption that only the respondent's own attributes have an effect, nothing else: not his friends' types of employment nor his extended social networks (as in Mark Granovetter's *Getting a Job* model) nor such "market" contexts as proportions of various types of jobs available in his locality.

But as early as the 1970s, an important line of research began to argue that workers were grouped into sectors and that that sectoral context had a major effect not only on absolute achievement but also on the ways in which education, occupation, and so on *determined* that achievement. That sectoral tradition is well illustrated by E. M. Beck, Patrick Horan, and Charles Tolbert's "Stratification in a Dual Economy." The paper predicts annual earnings based on the usual array of variables: sex, race, age, education, occupational prestige, union membership, work stability, and parents' schooling and occupation. What is unusual is that the data (national survey data) are split into "core" and "periphery" sectors by the individuals' type of employment. The equations were estimated separately for the two sectors, and tests were then done to see whether the effects varied between the two sectors. The paper finds that not only are rewards vastly different in the two sectors but so also is the size of the effects of various variables on those rewards. Context matters. The individuals should not be seen as an undifferentiated mass but rather as grouped into these two quite separate labor markets.

Note that this paper could also be seen as employing the splitting heuristic of the last chapter. The context is not particularly elaborate; it's simply a matter of seeing the workers in two groups. A clearer example is "The Population Ecology of Organizations" by Michael Hannan and John Freeman, which launched an entire paradigm of organizational analysis. I have already mentioned this celebrated paper as an example of borrowing. What was borrowed was a model of context. Rather than thinking of organizations standing alone, Hannan and Freeman argued, we should imagine them in a competitive ecology. Rather than thinking of them as adapting consciously to environmental opportunities and threats, we should think of them as constrained and unable to adapt, their future determined in fact by the competitive pressures of their peers. Employing formal models borrowed directly from biology, Hannan and Freeman proposed that we recast our theory of organizations entirely.

Like the Lorrain and White paper mentioned above, the Hannan and Freeman paper included many formalities that the later literature discarded. But at the heart of the article was an insistence on context as *the* most important determinant of an organization's trajectory. Not surprisingly, researchers following in this tradition studied the founding and dissolution of organizations extensively and sought to put into practice concepts like niche and generalist. Later on, the radical contextualism of the initial theoretical formulation was lost; routine methods that had not been conspicuously contextualized (durational methods) emerged as the standard methodology for population-ecology studies. We should recall, however, that the tradition began with a radical contextualizing move, invoked in the context of formal methods, where such moves were unusual.

Another elegant illustration of contextualizing, from yet another tradition of methods, is Elizabeth Bott's "Urban Families," a shortened version of what became her book *Family and Social Network*. Bott's paper has close ties to several literatures we have encountered, in particular, the literatures on social networks and on the household division of labor. Her research was done under the auspices of the Tavistock Institute in London, a research center dedicated largely to psychological investigations. Her original aim was to "further the sociological and psychological understanding of families," and her research design—intensive study of twenty families—bore witness to that interest in depth of analysis.

The research itself resulted in an extraordinary conclusion: the family division of labor was very closely related not to the psychological qualities of the husband or the wife or both but rather to the degree of connectedness of the family's social network. Bott did not find the strong "subculture" pattern mentioned in my discussion of George Farkas's paper. Although professional families tended to have more jointness and sharing of household tasks than families of lower social status, there were plenty of exceptions and counterexamples. What did turn up as an absolute regularity was that families with strong role separation had tight, fully connected social networks around them. Again, context mattered.

Bott did not specify which way causality ran, although her argument leans toward saying that the networks determined the household divisions of labor rather than vice versa. What is important for us is that rather than following Tavistock's bent for psychological or psychodynamic explanation, Bott turned outward, to social connections—social context—in her attempt to discover the origins of the household division of labor. It is instructive that when Farkas did his quantitative paper more than twenty years later, this move toward context had been forgotten.

We should not think that moves are always made toward context, however. Sometimes it is essential to resist the pressure to study context. We are most familiar with this, as I said, as a strain in SCA and formalization. But the anticontextual impulse is fairly common in history as well. There it takes the form of going back to raw documents and rediscovering history from the documents up.

An excellent recent example of this is Amanda Vickery's extraordinary *Gentleman's Daughter*. Vickery wanted to know what really happened to genteel women in the eighteenth century. General accounts of women in this period have emphasized the removal of women from their role in production, the creation of "idle domesticity," and the rise of "separate spheres" for men and women. Vickery attacked this tradition on several grounds. First, scholars have traced these developments to wildly varying periods between the sixteenth and nineteenth centuries. Second, these arguments usually originate in the simple (and erroneous) deduction that some kind of gradual transition must exist between the starting point of the medieval productive family and the end point of the late-nineteenth-century system of absolutely separate spheres. Scholars deduced this transition and then imposed it on data. Indeed, Vickery also attacks the methodological roots of these accounts, which are usually based on print sources (which are highly selective). She also notes that the urge to locate family trends with respect to related political and economic contexts has led to an arguing *from* contextual evidence (about politics, say, or production in the industrial revolution) *to* the family (as in the assumption that as production moved out of the household into factories, women *must* have played a smaller role in it). Note that these arguments use a wide variety of heuristic moves in addition to the contextualizing one.

Vickery sets aside contextual phenomena such as the rise of consumption, the transformation of the economy, and the remaking of social life. She also sets aside the "larger" history of England in the eighteenth century. Robert Walpole, the Pitts, the Seven Years' War, the American War of Independence, the industrial revolution—these, too, are nearly absent. Rather, she starts with the immediate situation itself, with thousands of pages of diaries and letters written by more than one hundred women (and a few men) in the north of England. And from these myriad details, she builds up a complex picture of the everyday world of these women, under the headings "gentility," "love and duty," "fortitude and resignation," "prudent economy," "elegance," "civility and vulgarity," and "propriety." Of course, the women are seen in extraordinary *local* contextual detail. But we see the larger context only as *they* saw it. We see only what the documents discuss. That eliding of larger events is indeed part of the book's empirical message, part of characterizing the world of experience these women knew.

In some ways, then, what the book does is exchange one set of contexts (the larger social processes seen by theorists) for another (the experiential contexts of everyday life: neighborhood, friends, correspondents, retailers, and so on). In this sense, historians never fully decontextualize. What results is a book of extraordinary strength of detail, a book whose portrait of women's lives utterly resists being assembled into larger arguments. Again and again, Vickery finds a middle way between the poles of prominent theoretical debates. On marriage, for example, she concludes:

> Marriage carried the potential both for harmonious license and for miserable servitude, as it long had done. The patriarchal and the companionate marriage were not successive stages in the development of the modern family, as Lawrene Stone has asserted, rather these were, as Keith Wrightson has sensibly argued, "poles of an enduring continuum in marital relations in a society which accepted both the primacy of male authority and the ideal of marriage as a practical and emotional partnership." (Vickery 1998:86)

By removing women's experience from the grasp of general arguments, as well as from important areas of political and social history, and taking it on its own terms as experience, Vickery both decontextualizes and recontextualizes. The result is to make the book hard to summarize and reduce to an abstract finding that can be inserted into theoretical debates about family and gender in Europe. This example makes it especially clear that the issue of context is always complex. Most removals from one context are attempts to emphasize another. When you use the contextualizing/noncontextualizing heuristic, you must indeed be deeply aware of this multiplicity of contexts. Even the most apparently noncontextualizing of SCA work is still situating its subjects somewhere.

VII. CHOICE AND CONSTRAINT

With choice and constraint, we come to a heuristic pairing that rises in what I have called problematics, the things we tend to take as problematic in the world. Some people think the world is to be understood in terms of choices, some in terms of constraints. As I noted in introducing this debate in Chapter Two, the opposition of choice and constraint tends to pit economists against many other social scientists. But I wish to rescue this debate, too, as a fruitful source of heuristic moves.

I shall illustrate the power of this heuristic by discussing some particularly extraordinary work done with choice and constraint in recent social science. One such example is the attempt of economists to develop an economic model of addiction. Addiction is a conundrum for economics because it seems to involve the choice of a behavior known to have negative rewards. Economists have tried to account for it by setting a high discount rate for rewards, so that the near-term pleasures of addiction—even if they are small—overwhelm the far-off (and possibly large) costs because those costs are discounted in value the further off they are. Such a model, although preserving the concept of choice even in so unpromising a field as addiction, does not effectively explain the fact that addicts often try to limit their future behavior.

In a brilliant argument, the psychologist George Ainslie has shown that we can account for addictive behaviors and other kinds of "temporary preferences" if we are willing to create a "picoeconomics" inside the individual (1992), a mini-economics differing from standard economics in two ways. First, it is governed not by the standard choice rules and discounting curves of the economists but by different rules and a different kind of discounting (hyperbolic rather than exponential). Second, the "actors" in this picoeconomics are not individuals but successive motivational states, with their interests varying according to the future periods they govern. The addict's internal life is then an economic arena in which the long-run selves and the short-run self compete to "buy" the "reward" of his behaving according to the wishes of one of them as opposed to another. The multiple internal states sustain the possibility of ambivalence, and hyperbolic discount curves, which can cross each other in ways that exponential ones cannot, guarantee the creation of the "temporary preferences" toward which the addict is ambivalent.

This model thus "outchoiced" the economists by turning their rational individual into a little economy of choices, although choices obeying somewhat different rules from those of standard economics. Ainslie came to this argument over a long period of time, of course. (He was not addicted to the short-term pleasure of writing attacks on economists but took nearly twenty years to assemble the entire argument into a book.) His move shows the power of introducing even more choice into a system already deeply committed to choice as a model of affairs.

At the same time, others have of course tried to suggest limited forms of constraints on choice. As I have mentioned several times, Herbert Simon's work is associated with the notion of "bounded rationality" (1982). It starts out from choice-based models of human affairs, then inquires into the impact of constraints on them. Among these, the most important and most studied involve information: you can't always get enough information to make a "rational decision," and the information you do get costs you something, which must be taken out of your total reward. A large literature has examined these "bounds of rationality."

The vacillation between moves toward choice and moves toward constraint is characteristic of stratification literature as well. Some who have studied the status-attainment process have ignored the constraints posed to mobility by the availability of jobs; others have not. Blau and Duncan's *American Occupational Structure*, frequently mentioned in these pages, ultimately takes little notice of the constraints on mobility choices. By contrast, the segmented-labor-market literature developed a strong focus on constrained mobility between the primary and secondary labor markets. Writers like Seymour Spilerman (1977) focused on the career as a sequence of the results of many constrained choices over a lifetime. Indeed, some writers try to envision the interlocking of two choices: choice of job by person and choice of person by job. This is the theme of the "job matching" literature in labor economics. What the diversity of this literature makes clear is that a very useful heuristic indeed is to question the role of choice and constraint in one's research problem. Thinking about these in new ways can open up whole new terrains for investigation and research.

VIII. Conflict and Consensus

The pairing of conflict and consensus also has its uses as a heuristic. Most of us have pretty clear preferences on this one, and it is both useful and important to try to rearrange them. Adherents of the two poles differ in their view of human nature, in where they think conflict comes from, and in what they think are the effects of conflict. Consensus thinkers hold that people are disorderly and greedy and that social conflict comes from these qualities of human nature. They are not interested in where conflict comes from (that is obvious to them) but only in how it is to be restrained or contained. By contrast, conflict thinkers hold that people are by nature orderly and that social conflict is foisted on people by wrongful social institutions.

Their research seeks the origins of those institutions. When we put it this baldly, the contrast seems extreme, but the pieces of it do make up useful heuristic choices, as some examples will make clear.

Perhaps the most famous examples of work playing with the conflict and consensus debate come from the many writers who have studied, in Gerald Suttles's words, *The Social Order of the Slum*. The classic theory of slums, inherited from turn-of-the-century progressivism, is that they are places without a social order. In them, the raw forces of untamed human nature run free. With no social control to restrain them, these forces produce the disorders so feared by urban reformers: poverty, hopelessness, crime, divorce, and so on. This was an absolute consensus position.

But William F. Whyte's brilliant *Street Corner Society* showed that Boston's North End, so feared by city leaders, was in fact a highly orderly community with its own elaborate rules and institutions. Whyte studied bowling leagues among the "corner boys" and found that boys' bowling scores correlated exactly with their social status, maintained by implicit rules and controls. He examined the numbers game (an illegal lottery on horse races) and found it to be a steady employer and stabilizing community influence. He studied local politics and found that its corruption played an important role in facilitating and regularizing community life. In short, he found a highly orderly social system, one with functioning institutions and rules that were simply a little different from the rules of the nonimmigrant community. Suttles's *Social Order of the Slum* did the same thing for a more complex neighborhood, with three ethnic groups, on Chicago's Near West Side in the 1960s.

Again, underneath the disorder so emphasized in consensus views of city structure was an elaborate and complex set of social rules—different, to be sure, but elaborate and extremely strong.

By contrast, Mark Suchman and Mia Cahill, writing about lawyers in California's Silicon Valley in the 1990s (1996), faced a different situation. Here, the standard view of the situation was a conflict-theory one. Lawyers were widely regarded in the literature as disturbing influences who introduced adversarialism and got in the way of simple market relationships. Entrepreneurs and venture capitalists, in this view, would get along fine if their lawyers weren't introducing so much complexity, formality, and contentiousness into relationships that had been smooth, informal, and relatively unconflicted. Suchman interviewed dozens of entrepreneurs, lawyers, and others and found that far from introducing disorder, lawyers were in fact among the most important *facilitators* of entrepreneurial life in Silicon Valley. Their contingent fee structures reduced important uncertainties for entrepreneurs. Their opinion letters helped manage uncertainties for investors. They served as gatekeepers and builders for the informal funding and entrepreneurial networks that built the community. In short, where the conflict theorists had seen lawyers as a disturbing force, Suchman and Cahill—taking a more consensual point of view—saw them as an essential ordering institution of the community.

So in both cases, we have authors who moved toward seeing order where others saw disorder, but in the first case the others were a body of *consensus* thinkers and in the second a body of *conflict* thinkers. The same move—but in two quite different intellectual contexts.

A different move is made by James Kuklinski and his colleagues in an influential paper on political tolerance (1991). This paper, like most of the literature on political tolerance, is built on a consensus framework. It assumes that people have strong likes and dislikes and that such institutions as tolerance, deliberation, and civil liberties are necessary to keep those likes and dislikes from excessive and destructive expression. Kuklinski and his colleagues start with a culture-to-behavior move, insisting that we must survey not just respondents' likes and dislikes of different groups but also their views of groups' potential acts. So the questions included not just "do you approve of Communists?" (or the Ku Klux Klan or whomever) but also "would you approve of the Communists' holding a rally?" (or the Klan, or whoever, holding a rally or teaching a class, or whatever). But Kuklinski and his colleagues also introduced diverse instructions to subjects. Some subjects received no instructions on how to answer, some were told to answer from the gut, without reflection, and some were told to think carefully about the consequences of the actions involved. It turned out that reflection strongly *reduced* tolerance.

The move here, then, was to investigate empirically whether one of the crucial "restraining" institutions of a consensus system actually supported that system. What turned out was that two important "consensus" values, tolerance and deliberation, seem to be in conflict. The heuristic move was not so much toward a conflict theory as it was a simple empirical questioning of the bases of a consensus theory.

An equivalent move on the conflict side is made in Ronald Coase's "Nature of the Firm," a paper that many decades after its publication was recognized as one of the classic papers of the century in economics. It starts with one of my earlier heuristics, asking, "Why are there firms?" Put a little more completely, it asks, "If the price mechanism and the market are so perfect, why should we organize *any* activities in another way—by command and nonmarket coordination, as we do in firms?" This is problematizing the obvious. Classical economics usually took firms for granted. Coase did not. But the way in which he proceeded fit the conflict/consensus heuristic quite nicely.

Classical microeconomics in some ways squares the conflict/consensus circle. On the one hand, it assumes people are greedy, as in consensus theory. On the other, it argues, with conflict theory, that this (greedy) nature produces an optimal state of affairs in its "natural" state unless we muck it up with disorderly and wrongful institutions. It's not important here that we reconcile this apparent difficulty in the distinction between conflict and consensus. (My argument would be that "economic man" is only partly greedy, greedy in a controlled way; microeconomics tacitly assumes an enormous amount of control in economic relations.) Here, Coase plays with only the second, conflict side of economics. Are firms in fact disorderly and wrongful institutions, mucking up the optimal system of markets? Coase says no; firms exist because there are "costs" to using the price mechanism to make decisions. For example, there are the costs of writing contracts for purchase and sale. There are the costs of marketing goods and services. There are the costs of writing specific contracts for long-term needs that may turn out differently than initially imagined. In short, firms emerge, Coase says, because people choose to organize activities in the cheapest way possible, and sometimes the cheapest way is within firms. (He also carefully includes an argument for why we don't organize *everything* this way, of course.)

Thus, Coase saves the price mechanism as the absolute principle for resource allocation by saying that people sometimes choose on price grounds not to use the price mechanism. What appears to be a violation of the universality of price logics—the existence of firms—is on the contrary the clearest evidence of its operation at a deeper level. The price principle is recursive; it can even justify its own removal. In short, what appeared to be an irrational institution cluttering up the free flow of market-based interaction is not an irrational, disorder-creating institution. It is itself an expression of the free flow of price reasoning.

Coase, too, is thus playing with the parts of the conflict/consensus debate. The various examples here show how useful it can be to question one's beliefs about the orderliness or disorderliness of behavior, about the nature of institutions as means of control or disorder. This whole series of problems offers a wide variety of different ways to rethink one's research questions. Like all the other fractal debates, conflict/consensus proves useful heuristically.

IX. TRANSCENDENT AND SITUATED KNOWLEDGE

An enormous debate rages in social science over the question of whether knowledge is transcendent or situated. Much of this debate is driven by political concerns. But we are concerned here not with what drives this debate but with how the debate is, and can be, used as a heuristic. It is best to start with an understanding of how the political version operates in terms of heuristics.

The logic of much of contemporary social science research begins with the recognition that "X is true" has often meant, in social science, "X is true for white men of the middle class" (or, worse yet, "X is true for a few college students I talked to"). Thousands of researchers have insisted on investigating whether this or that truth holds up in other groups, be they women, blacks, Vietnamese immigrants, old people, working-class Latina mothers, or whomever. The heuristic moves of such work are fairly straightforward. The first step is to say that what appeared to be general knowledge is in fact situated or local knowledge. The second step is to seek other forms of local knowledge. Once such research makes the original move against transcendence, it usually moves directly into the realm of the additive heuristic: "X was true there; is X true here?" Most often, it finds a negative answer, which then presents an opportunity for a wide variety of heuristic possibilities.

But if the move against transcendence is by far the most common of heuristic moves employing the situated/transcendent debate, there are some others as well, and it is useful to illustrate them.

I shall use two simple illustrations, both famous and classic papers about issues of transcendence. The first is one of the most influential papers in the literature on stress, the endlessly cited "Social Readjustment Rating Scale" (SRRS) article of Thomas Holmes and Richard Rahe. This paper is a classic because it made a very big bet on transcendence. Decades of clinical research had uncovered a long list of crucial events that shaped people's lives. It was obvious from this work that for any one of these life events, "the psychological significance and emotions varied widely with the patient" (1967:216). But the list was eventually given as a rating task ("how important is this event on a scale of 1 to 100?") to a large and fairly diverse sample of people. The results were averaged as a rating scale. The crucial move was as follows:

> Although some of the discrete subgroups do assign a different order and magnitude to the items, it is the degree of similarity between the populations in the sample that is impressive. The high degree of consensus also suggests a universal agreement between groups and among individuals about the significance of the life events under study that transcends differences in age, sex, marital status, education, social class, generation American, religion and race. (1967:217)

Holmes and Rahe bet on transcendence (as did Hodge, Siegel, and Rossi in the occupational-prestige paper mentioned earlier in this chapter). The subsequent literature employing these scale values is enormous, even though the issue of the variation that was ignored remains for investigation. The strength of a bet on transcendence is that it can produce such an enormous amount of interesting work. The danger is that we don't know exactly what that work is worth because we have lost sight of the variation it decided to ignore. Note, by the way, that the authors were perfectly aware of what they were doing. Indeed, the SRRS was backed up by a long *clinical* (that is, ethnographic) tradition going back to the great turn-of-the-century psychiatrist Adolf Meyer. Most of those who *used* the SRRS lacked that awareness, of course. This is a long-term danger; knowledge becomes ungrounded. But from our point of view, past bets on transcendence are always ripe targets for the situated-knowledge heuristic. What *were* those systematic variations Holmes and Rahe noticed? Have they gotten bigger with time? Are there subpopulations that really differ sharply? Every move on this scale creates opportunities to move in the opposite direction.

My second example is another famous bet on transcendence, but one that argues paradoxically that because a fact is transcendent, it is actually unimportant from a research point of view. In "Age and the Explanation of Crime," one of the classics of modern criminology, Travis Hirschi and Michael Gottfredson argued that the relationship between age and crime is so systematic and so invariant that there is no point in doing research that looks at variables that explain the distribution of age and crime. Since the distribution doesn't vary anywhere, it can't be explained by things that do. This paper is a quite unusual type: the definitively negative paper. For our purposes, what is striking about it is that rather than making a transcendence argument in order to facilitate further work—the common move, illustrated by the Holmes and Rahe paper just discussed—it essentially makes a transcendence argument to strike down further research. Age, Hirschi and Gottfredson say, is more or less uninteresting with respect to crime because its relationship to crime is completely invariant.

WITH MY DISCUSSION of the transcendent/situated debate and its associated heuristic moves, I come to the end of my discussion of fractal heuristics. My aim here has been to show how these profound debates, which generate so much noise and excitement in writing about paradigms and presuppositions, are, from the student's point of view, tools with which to generate hundreds of new ideas and arguments. An astonishing number of important pieces of social science have made their mark precisely by playing with these various debates in exciting ways. There is no reason the student should not use the same tools. You should get a sense of these debates and, above all, a sense of them not as something to get right or take a position on or otherwise etch in stone but as something to play with. These debates are the most sophisticated tools for producing new social science. And any good student can get in on the action.

Chapter Seven
IDEAS AND PUZZLES

WE HAVE NOW BEEN THROUGH four chapters of heuristics that generate new ideas. But not all of these new ideas will be good ideas. How do we know which are good and which are bad?

Part of the answer depends on what we mean by a good idea. Sometimes "good idea" means an idea worth retaining for the moment. (And it's worth remembering "the moment" could mean a lot of different things—five minutes, an afternoon, until I think of something better, and so on.) But sometimes a "good idea" means good on some absolute scale. A good idea is good because it's right or because we really believe it. Obviously, an idea has to see some testing before we decide it's good in this second sense.

There are several different ways to recognize and develop good ideas when we see them. First come tests we set ourselves. Critique starts at home, as everyone knows. So we need to discuss some personal ways to test ideas, to get a personal sense of whether they are worth elaborating and developing. Second come interactional tests, ways of trying the idea out on others. The usual ways of trying out our ideas on others are pretty wasteful. In the classroom and out of it, we often behave as if our ideas were weapons and others' ideas were targets. We dismiss them with the obligatory "that may be, but I think . . ." But intellectual life is neither a shoot-out nor a sequence of random opinions. It is a mutual challenge, with equal emphasis on *mutual* and *challenge*. Others' thoughts can help you see what's good and what's bad about your own.

Finally, we need to test our ideas with respect to existing scholarly writing on a topic. If you recall, I said at the outset that this book originated in the complaint I heard from many students that "I have nothing new to say." Now that you've read a book's worth of ways to find new ideas, the literature should no longer seem so frighteningly complete and comprehensive. So you're ready to use the literature in order to evaluate and develop your ideas. You have to understand how social scientific literatures work if you want to have ideas that make sense to the people who write them.

This leads us naturally to two broader topics: how we develop good taste in ideas and how we come to know our intellectual personalities. The question of taste is crucial. In the long run, good intellectual taste is the best passport to good ideas. But a passport is no good without a means of travel. So our personalities are equally important. Each of us has habits of thought that make certain ways of thinking more dangerous or more useful or more easy. These two topics, of taste and personality, bring me, finally, to the issue of puzzlement. Having good ideas also means being able to see certain things in the social world as puzzling. Cultivating puzzlement is my concluding concern.

I. TESTS OF IDEAS

Obviously, the first test of an idea is to try it out, to run it past some data. In practice, most ideas come from looking at data in the first place. Only when one is using formal methods do ideas come from dataless thinking, and even with formal methods the ideas usually come more from reflecting on commonsense knowledge than from pure deduction. Most people get their stimulus from thinking about data they've already got or empirical things they already know.

Once you've got an idea, you need to try it out on some new data. So if you're an ethnographer studying welfare-to-work training programs and you've begun to notice that the trainer's rhetoric emphasizes getting rid of race-stereotyped mannerisms, you start looking for other indications of overt or covert race retraining in other parts of your data. If you are Barrington Moore studying the histories of the revolutions that led to modernity and you notice that in America and France the old rural aristocracy was undercut completely but in Germany it survived and even dominated politics, you start looking for other cases and see if you can predict whether a government turns fascist based on how its rural aristocracy fared during modernization.

It's not just a matter of looking for other cases of a phenomenon or a relationship you've identified. It's also a question of looking for other implications that your idea has for data. Suppose you're a survey analyst studying married women's labor-force participation and you suddenly get the idea that it's driven by a woman's need to guarantee a skill set and an experience record so that she can support herself in case of divorce. You can infer from that idea that the long-term overall trend in women's labor-force participation should correlate closely with the long-term overall trend in the divorce rate. That correlation follows logically from your new idea because if women aren't more likely to get divorced (and to suffer divorce's economic loss), then (on your argument) there's not the same necessity for them to have work skills as a precaution. You also know that your idea implies (at the individual level) that women with alternative resources unaffected by divorce (women with inherited wealth, say) won't have to get the resources through work, and so your theory implies that they will be less likely to work (which they will also be for other reasons, of course). Both of these empirical predictions can be tested, formally or informally.

We see this deriving of implications most clearly in formal methods, for these usually produce clear predictions. The formal arguments in Schelling's famous *Micromotives* book have clear implications for traffic jams, for social movements and riots, and so on. Indeed, one could say the greatest virtue of formal methods is their copious production of implications.

But all ideas have implications for data, whatever the method used. You should get into the habit of continually generating these implications and of continually moving your ideas on to new cases or data. It should become a matter of second nature, something that goes on almost automatically when you think up an idea. My friend and colleague the late Roger Gould was a master at this. You would utter an idle truism, like "young people are always each other's harshest critics," and he immediately would respond, "Well, if that's true, then it ought to be the case that dissertation defenses will be easier on graduate students than having lunch with their friends" or "Do you really mean that people's harshest critics are always their peers, so that older people's harshest critics are other older people?" and so on. Note that just because an idea fails a few of these tests—makes a few bad predictions, doesn't work in a couple of cases—doesn't mean that we must throw it out. Most often, we get new wrinkles in our ideas that way; we learn how to move them around a bit, expand one part at the expense of another. (That's what Roger would have been suggesting by making the generalization that peers are always the harshest critics.) It's rather like decorating a room; you try it, step back, move a few things, step back again, try a serious reorganization, and so on.

This continuous monitoring and testing of your ideas rests more than anything else on a firm command of logic. The basic logical forms—implication, inverse, converse, and so on—need to be hardwired into your mind so that the process of monitoring goes on in the background, like the antivirus software on your computer. It is a matter of practice as much as anything else. If your logic software hasn't been updated recently, a review might be worthwhile. Being able to quickly think up three or four implications (positive and negative) of a social theory is a crucial skill.

In order to be tested, all of these ideas and implications must be framed in such a way that they can be wrong. It is great if your idea works most of the time, but if it works all the time, you should start to suspect it. It's likely to be a truism and therefore not terribly interesting. (Although sometimes it's fun to turn a truism on its head, as we've seen.) It is quite surprising how many researchers—even graduate students in their dissertations—propose arguments that can't be wrong. For example, research proposals of the form "I am going to take a neo-institutionalist view of mental-hospital foundings" or "This paper analyzes sexual insults by combining a Goffmanian account of interaction and a semiotic approach to language" are not interesting because they do not propose an idea that can be wrong. They boil down to classifying a phenomenon or, seen the other way around, simply illustrating a theory.

Similarly, universal predicates are in general uninteresting, even if they are consequential. Thus, the idea that this or that aspect of reality—gender roles, say, or accountancy—is socially constructed is not particularly interesting. Everything is socially constructed in some sense, and probably even in a relatively strong sense. The interesting questions involve *how* gender roles are socially constructed or *what the consequences* of the constructed nature of accounting experts are. Watch out for universal predicates.

Another way to put this is to say that good ideas have real alternatives, not simple negations. It is better to be thinking "A is true or B is true" than "A is true or A is not true." If you have a genuine puzzle, you want to solve it, not simply to know that one particular solution doesn't work. Thinking without alternatives is a particular danger in ethnography and historical analysis, where the natural human desire to develop cohesive interpretations (and the need to present a cohesive interpretation at the end of the research) prompts us to notice only those aspects of reality that accord with our current ideas. It's also surprisingly common in standard quantitative work, which often tests ideas against things that are called, all too literally, null hypotheses. The majority of published quantitative articles do *not* have two real alternatives that are *both* dear to the writer. Most of the time, the writer's sympathies are clear well ahead of time, and the suspense is purely rhetorical. The writer's ideas are tested against random chance, even though nobody really thinks pure randomness occurs much in social life. All of this is wrong. An idea always does its best if it has a real alternative. Always maintain *two* basic ideas about your project, and try to be equally attached to both.

Truisms are not a lost cause, however. It is a useful challenge to try to make a truism into an idea that can be wrong. Suppose we wanted to make something out of the old joke that the leading cause of divorce is marriage. To make this meaningful, one has only to reconceptualize marriage as formalization of a relationship and divorce as breakup or damage, and we have the very interesting hypothesis that formalizing a love relationship decreases some aspect of its quality and hence makes it more likely to dissolve. This, too, is a platitude (not only in the nontechnical literature on romance but also in Weber's formal version of it as "routinization of charisma"), but it is not definitionally true and could be empirically right or wrong. It's a much better idea than the bald statement that "marriage is the leading cause of divorce," if a little less amusing.

Not being able to be wrong is thus a sign of a bad idea. It goes without saying that having no empirical referent at all is also a sign of a bad idea. An idea of the form "The population-ecology theory of organizations is really just a version of conflict theory" is not very interesting. One could for various reasons want to write a polemical paper about it, but it's not a powerful or exciting idea, unless we turn it into the empirical assertion that "the population-ecology theory of organizations *arose historically from* conflict theory." Although somewhat vague, this version has the beginnings of a good idea in it. The first version is just a classificatory exercise. The second is an empirical assertion about the history of social science.

A good idea, then, ought to have some referent in the real world. This is not to deny the utility of pure social theory, but the vast majority of social theory consists of relabeling. All real theory arises in empirical work, in the attempt to make sense of the social world, no matter how abstractly construed. A student is well advised to stay clear of writing pure theory. It's an open invitation to vacuity.

To pursue this argument a bit, we should note that it is also a bad sign if an idea works too well or too quickly. Usually this means that the idea is just *relabeling* something that is already known or accepted. When you have an idea—say, that a certain kind of behavior is guided by norms—most of the time you are simply relabeling the fact that the behavior is regular and consistent. The notion of norms doesn't add anything to the fact of regularity unless it involves the positive assertion that the regularity is produced by obligatory, emergent rules. But then you have the problem of demonstrating that these rules actually exist independent of the behavior they enjoin. It's this existence question that is crucial, and if you don't fight it out, your work is just providing fancy labels for something simple.

Relabeling is a general activity in social science because it's a way of appearing novel without having to do much. Often when you've just read a new theorist, that theorist's language will seem supremely compelling because of its novelty, but then it will turn out to be the same old stuff with new names. Much of sociology fell in love with Pierre Bourdieu's word *practice*, for example, but most of the time when the term is used by others in sociology, it simply means "regular behavior." It's just a new word for something we have talked about for a long time. To the extent that it *is* new, it involves the assertion that the behavior involved is in some way self-perpetuating, that doing it regularly creates the possibility and the likelihood that we will do it even more. That is a stronger assertion—one that must be considered empirically—but of course it, too, is quite old and familiar. (Stinchcombe called this mechanism "historicist explanation," for example [1968].)

Ideas that reclassify something are also usually pretty uninteresting. "Social work is really a profession" is an interesting topic polemically, but as a research idea it is going to be interesting only if by seeing social work as a profession, we can understand something profoundly puzzling about it. For example, we might think that demonstrating that social work was really a profession might explain why its practitioners work for so little money. But then the strong form of the idea would be some more general statement, such as "People are always willing to exchange prestige for salary, and being thought professional confers high prestige." This is quite different from "Social work is really a profession." By themselves, then, classificatory ideas aren't interesting, but they often conceal an interesting question. So the proper challenge to present to a classificatory idea is Why do I think this classification matters? What is really at issue? Note, too, that in the largest scale, reclassifications are often analogies, which are among the most powerful of heuristic gambits. Saying that the family was really a utility-maximizing unit like any other helped win Gary Becker the Nobel Prize in economics.

The criteria for good ideas discussed so far are short-term criteria. These are not the only ones. One of the most important tests of a good idea, needless to say, is that it still seems like a good idea when you get up the next day or when you've been doing something else for a few days and come back to it. This seems obvious enough, but in practice we often forget it. For from this obvious fact follows the corollary that no good paper is ever written at a single sitting, the practice of generations of college students (including me) notwithstanding. If you don't go away from an idea—really go away from it, so that you've forgotten important parts of it—you can't come back to it with that outsider's eye that enables you to see whether it's good or not. A good idea is one that stays faithful even when you go out with other ideas. There's no other way to test that than to do it.

In the long haul, the best personal criterion for a good idea is the one presented by the philosopher Imre Lakatos thirty years ago (1970). A good idea is one that is "nondegenerating." It is productive. It gives rise to more ideas, to more puzzles, to more possibilities. Its curve is upward. At the same time, it doesn't deceive us with the "suddenly everything is solved" feeling that comes from truisms and relabelings. A good idea is a little resistant to us. It sometimes doesn't work when we want it to and sometimes it works when we least expect it to.

Ultimately, one knows good ideas by the solid feeling they give over time. A good idea will make you feel secure while you do the grunt work that takes up the majority of research time: cleaning quantitative data, spending lonely time in ethnographic settings, slogging through archival documents. When you do these things with a good idea in your head, you know why you are doing them. That gives you the confidence and endurance you otherwise lack. When you don't have a guiding idea, you feel desperate; you hope that somehow an idea will emerge magically from the next page of coefficients, the next incomprehensible document or conversation. Indeed, students often throw themselves into the detail work to hide from their feeling that there isn't a big idea. Don't. Work at the idea, and the grunt work will become much more bearable.

II. OTHER PEOPLE

Once an idea has passed our own preliminary screening, it needs to be tried out on others. Sometimes this exercise will be formal, sometimes informal.

From the start, trying out ideas on others is different from trying them out on yourself. Others do not hear your ideas the way you hear them yourself. It's not just that they disagree or something like that. Rather, inside our own heads, our ideas are sustained by a lot of assumptions and things taken for granted that we are unaware of. It's like singing. Any instrument but the voice is heard by performer and listener in the same way: through the ear. But your voice reaches your ear as much through the inner passages of the head as through the outer ear, so it never sounds the same to you as to someone else. That's why singers are always listening to recordings of themselves, trying to hear what others hear.

So, too, with ideas. They never sound the same to others. And it is crucial to remember that for all save a handful of us, it is their sound to others that matters: to teachers, to readers, to professional or popular audiences we may wish to persuade. The more arrogant among us find this a hard lesson to learn. You can say things in ways that *you* find perfect, insightful, brilliant. But if other people don't or can't hear them when you present them, you must find a better way to communicate. Otherwise, you will be ignored.

Saying that your own ideas don't sound the same to others is a way of saying that you will always find yourself leaving out crucial aspects of your idea when you talk to other people. Indeed, it is by carefully listening to what other people say in response to your idea—what they add, what they want clarified, what they misunderstand—that you will be able to figure out the essential and inessential parts of the idea. So listen carefully to others' demands for clarification.

At the same time, however, it is true that an idea that requires a *huge* amount of explanation is probably not a good idea. Most likely, it just doesn't work, and the need for explanation is telling you that. Note that these two arguments push in different directions. The first says you should figure out from others what you need to explain or add or remove in order to make your idea work. On that argument, the more problems others have with your idea, the more you can figure out about it. The second says that if you have to do too much explaining, your idea probably isn't good; the more problems other people have with it, the weaker your idea is. The skill of learning from other people—and it is a skill, just like any other—lies in figuring out how to read these two contradictory processes correctly.

The first is the more important of the two. No matter how smart you are, always assume that if other people can't understand you, it's not due to their stupidity, disinterest, envy, and so on, but to your inability to articulate your idea properly. The reason for making this assumption is not that it is necessarily correct; they may well be stupid, disinterested, and so on. But the assumption enables you to get the maximum out of them. Every social scientist learns this from dealing with blind referees (people who review articles for publication in journals; usually they are unidentified colleagues at other universities). One's first reaction to their criticisms is to scream and yell in anger. But even if they *are* fools, the way they misunderstood you tells you how to write better for others.

Some of us don't get angry at negative comments. We find them overwhelming and collapse before them. But even if you *believe* someone who says your idea is junk, you should assume that the reason this smart person thought your idea was wrong was that you didn't say it right, not that the idea itself is bad. That enables you to use others' comments to improve your idea, to raise it to its highest possible level. It may turn out to be much better than you think.

The things you learn from this process of clearing up others' presumed misunderstandings are fairly specific. You learn first about intermediate steps that you left out of your argument; these are hidden stages you may not have noticed and may involve real difficulties. You also learn about the background assumptions that you make—often as part of your general way of thinking about the world—that others do not necessarily share. If you are careful, you will also learn a great deal about the specific (and often contradictory) meanings that people give to words. For example, I called my book about professions *The System of Professions*, more or less because I liked the sound of that title, which I used for an early paper on the subject. Knowing my book had a title allowed me to feel it was more real somehow during the five years it took to write it. But I have since discovered that many people infer from the word *system* that the book argues that there is some kind of grand intention behind the way professions work, as if all of society's professions were part of a huge plan. In fact, the book says precisely the reverse of that, but I had forgotten what the word *system* means to most readers. Thus, one should remember that social science is a place where most of the basic concepts— identity, structure, culture, nation, and so on—do not have anything like generally accepted definitions. Indeed, this is *always* the first place to look for misunderstanding: the definitions of the words you are using to state your idea.

Note that I haven't said much yet about whether other people think your idea is good. I have talked only about the fact that they are likely to misunderstand it. It is important not to take other people's first reactions to your ideas at face value. This is true whether they think it's a great idea or a bad one. If they think it's great, it could easily be that they don't understand it any more than you do and that it's really a bad idea that you both have misunderstood. Or it could be that they don't really care much and are agreeing in order to be polite. Or it could be that you have an overbearing personality and they're agreeing because it's too much work for them to disagree. The same if they think it's a lousy idea: they could have misunderstood it altogether; they could have understood it but missed its greatness; they could be dismissive people who never agree with anyone but themselves. In sum, don't take the first few reactions seriously.

The first hint that you are past the stage of first reactions comes when you yourself feel confident that you can state your idea clearly, effectively, and *briefly*. The *crucial* moment comes when other people are able to *repeat* your idea to you in such a way that you recognize it and agree with their presentation of it. For an undergraduate trying out ideas for a course paper, this is going to happen after talking to four or five people and hammering out the details. For a graduate student writing a dissertation proposal, this is going to happen after many weeks and many drafts.

Whenever it comes, the ability of others to restate your idea clearly is the watershed. Then you can start to put some faith in their judgment. Of course, you still have to factor in their personalities. Arrogant people like only their own ideas. Negative people don't like anything. Pollyannas like everything. You have to reset your meter based on the person you're talking to. If the negativist thinks it is not the worst idea he or she has ever heard, maybe that's good news. This relativism is true, by the way, for faculty just as much as for anyone else; there are faculty of all types, from thoughtlessly arrogant to hopelessly negative to mindlessly supportive. Although only their own graduate students really know how to read particular faculty members, it's wise to be aware that each has a unique style. You can probably guess most of it, and you need to second-guess the rest.

You will find that it is useful to build up a small group of people who are sympathetic but thoughtfully critical. (The way to do this, of course, is to play the same role for them.) It's also important to keep peddling your ideas in many different places. Your friends get used to you (they start to know, and make up for, your hidden assumptions) and will ultimately get too easy on you. Finding a group of people who will listen to, read, and reflect on your developing ideas is the most important thing you can do. It is also the hardest.

For those who become serious scholars, the ultimate test of a good idea is the taxi-driver test. If you are on your way somewhere to present your idea and you cannot *in five sentences* explain what you are talking about well enough so that your taxi driver or the person in the adjacent aircraft seat can understand it and see why it's interesting, you don't really understand your idea yet. You aren't ready to present it. This holds no matter how complex your idea is. If you can't state it in everyday terms for an average person with no special interest in it, you don't understand it yet. Even for those working in the most abstruse formalisms, this is the absolute test of understanding.

III. LITERATURE

I have talked so far about submitting your ideas to your own judgment and your friends' judgment. But what about the relationship of a new idea to previous published work? For undergraduates, this is the hardest bit. It always seems that everything that could possibly be said has been said. There is no room to enter, no place to start. Moreover, when you do think up something startling and new, the literature's reaction (via the faculty) can be incomprehending or dismissive.

The first thing to realize is that it is probably true that everything that could be said has been said, at least at the level of generality at which an undergraduate is likely to be thinking. But this does not prevent faculty themselves from saying the same things again and again—but in new ways, with new evidence, in new contexts. Indeed, that's what a huge proportion of excellent social science scholarship is: saying the old things in new ways. (If we didn't say them again and again, we'd forget them, which would be a bad thing.) What faculty know that students do not know—and what enables them to accomplish this turning of old things into new ones—is the conventional nature of the literature. They know which old things can be resaid and, indeed, which old things *need* to be resaid. They know how the literature defines the border between restating something and stating something new.

This system of conventions is mostly invisible to undergraduates and even to most graduate students. Suppose you take a stratification course. You read the stratification literature. There are a lot of questions that occur to you about that literature that most people writing in it don't seem to worry about. For example, why should we judge somebody's success by how well he or she was doing in a particular year? Why should we assume that everybody judges success by the same scale? Why do we think about a family's social status by asking the job of the husband? Indeed, why is measuring social status more important than measuring, say, personal judgments of well-being or satisfaction? And so on. Occasionally, these things do get written about, of course. But in the main, the stratification literature goes on happily envisioning new puzzles and issues without thinking about these questions for a second. They are ignored by common agreement. Yet they seem of burning importance to an undergraduate, and rightly so.

As I have said throughout, literatures work by making simplifying assumptions about some things so that researchers can do complex analyses of other things. That's the nature of the beast. It's not possible to do social science—by any method whatsoever—without making simplifying assumptions. They facilitate research by preventing people from bogging down in preliminaries. So survey analysts make assumptions about how attitudes relate to behavior, and ethnographers make assumptions about how informants do and do not twist the truth. And such assumptions usually go well beyond the methodological preliminaries. They get into the very details of the substance, as I just noted in the case of stratification research.

Faculty know these conventions so well that they are usually quite unaware of them as conventions. As a result, many ideas that occur immediately to undergraduates seem ridiculous to faculty. "We showed years ago that that didn't matter," "That's more a question of method and technique than substance," and "That's really not what is central here" are typical reactions to what seem like obvious questions to a bright undergraduate. All of these may mean that the faculty member has forgotten that your idea is a legitimate question because it has been set aside conventionally by the literature. (These statements don't *necessarily* mean that, of course, but they may.)

Often, as we saw in Chapters Three through Six, a good idea is one that pushes one or another of these conventions. But a good idea doesn't try to push several conventions at once. So, to continue the stratification example, it would be interesting to ask what happens to the standard relationship between education and family social status if we used the wife's job prestige instead of the husband's as the indicator of family social status or if we used some average of both. Such a study would contribute to the literature precisely by opening up one of its conventional assumptions to further analysis. But suppose one changed indicators on *both* sides of the relationship, not only moving to the wife's job prestige as the status indicator but also changing education from degrees or years in school (the standard indicators) to a true outcome variable, like SAT scores, for example (on the assumption that the SAT actually measures prior achievement and schooling more than it measures schooling-independent talent). This would restrict one's attention to the college bound, as well as changing one's conceptual idea of the meaning of education. And now the study begins to lose its relation to the traditional stratification literature, where it is conventional to think about stratification in terms of breadwinner employment and where it is customary to consider education in terms of credentials (with their more direct link to occupation and income) rather than achievement scores (which measure a less actualized but perhaps more general resource). So you would have done a doubly brilliant study, but one hanging in midair as far as literatures are concerned.

Conventions play an important role in all methods and literatures. A historically inclined student might be interested in changes in the patterns of lawyers' careers over the twentieth century and decide to approach it by reading twenty or thirty biographies of lawyers in order to develop a schematic model of lawyers' lives. But a faculty adviser would probably make the largely conventional judgment that the student should move either toward a quantitative analysis, digging up simple information for a much larger but random sample of lawyers throughout the period, *or* toward a detailed study of two or three lawyers suitably spaced through the century. The convention is either to be fully scientific, with a defensible strategy and agreed-upon career measures, or to be deeply interpretive. Yet against the first plan, one could easily argue that changes in the nature of lawyers' jobs meant that coding categories, like "working for a law firm," meant something completely different in 1900 than they did in 2000; in that sense, there is no stable categorization of jobs that will enable meaningful coding over the century. And against the second plan, one could argue that its sampling is so arbitrary that any conclusions are spurious. Nonetheless, the conventions are that you probably can do the positivist version or the interpretive version, but you will have trouble writing about twenty to thirty lawyers' lives in the middle.

Dealing with conventions is another of these damned-if-you-do, damned-if-you-don't things. Everybody agrees that whatever else it does, the best work nearly always overturns some conventions. At the same time, the general preference is to obey conventions, especially when one is starting out. So you can obey the conventions and have people think you unadventurous or disobey them and have people reject or misunderstand what you are doing. For students, the best way to learn the research conventions is of course to look at current work, and the easiest way to generate feasible ideas is to clone an existing project by changing one detail: getting a new variable, changing the time period examined, adding some more cases. (This is the additive heuristic of Chapter Three.) But this invites the charge of timidity.

There is no way out of this dilemma, which is, after all, the dilemma of creativity in social science writ small. It is important, nonetheless, to know about the problem of conventions, because it is the key to understanding how the professionals in your world—meaning people who know a given area better than you do, be they older students or faculty—will react to your ideas. Often, faculty push students toward following conventions for the very good reason that unconventional work is much harder. Students' research plans are often unrealistic in the extreme, and faculty are trying to encourage students' interests while helping make the research more feasible. Urging students to learn conventional research models and to write conventional papers is a way of doing that. A student needs to be aware of this complex tension between convention, originality, and feasibility—and to be willing to make some compromises if necessary.

IV. TASTE

Conventions and the problem of knowing them bring us to the matter of taste. Judging one's ideas becomes much easier when one begins to acquire scholarly taste. By taste, I mean a general, intuitive sense of whether an idea is likely to be a good one or not. It is of course important not to become a slave of one's taste, to try new things as one tries new foods. But developing a sense of taste makes things a lot easier.

The foundation of good taste—like the foundation of good heuristic—is broad reading. It is not necessary that all the reading be of good material, only that it be broad and that it always involve judgment and reflection. A musical metaphor is again useful. A good pianist always practices not only technique and repertoire but also sight-reading. Broad reading for social scientists is the equivalent of sight-reading for pianists. A pianist practicing sight-reading grabs a random piece of music and reads it through, playing steadily on in spite of mistakes and omissions. So, too, should you just pick up pieces of social science or sociology or whatever and just read through them, whether you know the details of the methods, see the complexities of the argument, or even like the style of analysis. The obvious way to do this is to pick up recent issues of journals and quickly read straight through them.

You learn many things from such broad reading. You learn the zones of research in the discipline. You learn the conventions of each zone, and you figure out which you like and which you don't like. You learn what interests you and what does not. Of course, you should not let your interests dictate your reactions, just as you should disregard, when you are "sight-reading," conventions with which you disagree. When you find you don't like a paper's methodology and you think its concepts don't make sense, force yourself to go on and ask what there is that you *can* get out of it—perhaps some facts, a hypothesis, even (in the worst case) some references. In the best disciplinary journals, every article will have something to teach you, even those articles that lie completely outside your own preferences.

This is also a useful rule for seminars and lectures, which are another useful place to develop your taste. There is no point in sitting through a lecture or talk whose methods you hate, self-righteously telling yourself about the "positivist morons" or the "postmodern bullshit" or whatever. All that does is reinforce your prejudices and teach you nothing. Judge a talk or a paper with respect to what it is itself trying to do. This is hard, but by working at it, you will gain a much surer sense of both the strengths and the weaknesses of your own preferences. You will become able to gather useful ideas, theories, facts, and methodological tricks from material that used to tell you nothing.

You will, of course, run into plenty of bad stuff: bad books, bad papers, bad talks. The symptoms are usually pretty clear: pontification, confusion, aimlessness, overreliance on authorities. Other signs are excessive attention to methods rather than substance and long discussions of the speaker's or writer's positions on various important debates. But even bad material can teach you things. Most important, it can teach you how to set standards for an article or talk on its own terms. What was the writer trying to accomplish? For the truly terrible, what should the writer have been *trying* to accomplish? This last is the question that enables you to judge material on its own grounds, by imagining the task it should have set itself.

Of course, it is also important self-consciously to read good work. Oddly enough, good work will not teach you as much as will bad. Great social science tends to look self-evident after the fact, and when it's well written, you may not be able to see what the insight was that instituted a new paradigm. What you take away from good work is more its sense of excitement and clarity, its feeling of ease and fluidity. Not that these are very imitable. But they set an ideal.

How does one find such good work? At the start, you ask people you know—faculty members, friends, fellow students. You also look at influential material, although—again oddly—there is plenty of influential material that is badly argued and opaque. Soon your taste will establish itself, and you can rely more on your own judgment. There is no substitute for practice and, in particular, for "sight-reading." You just need to learn to read and make judgments, always working around your own prejudices to separate bad work from work you simply don't like.

Developing this taste about others' ideas is a crucial step toward judging your own. Even given all the hints scattered throughout this chapter, judging your own ideas is the hardest task of all. The only way to become skilled at it is to acquire general taste and then carefully and painfully turn that taste on your own thinking. The skill of learning to find good and bad things in the work of others can be the best help in finding the good and bad things in your own work.

V. Personality

Part of developing a taste for good ideas is getting a sense of your own strengths and weaknesses as a thinker. You must eventually learn to second-guess your scholarly judgments. This second-guessing comes from understanding your wider character as a researcher and thinker: your intellectual personality. Your intellectual personality is based on your everyday character, of course, but builds on it in surprising ways. The strengths and weaknesses of your intellectual character decisively influence the way you evaluate ideas and, indeed, everything about the way you think.

It is important to realize from the start that every aspect of your intellectual character, like every aspect of your everyday character, is both a strength and a weakness. In the everyday world, what is precious loyalty in one context is mindless obstinacy in another. The same two-facedness is true in the research world. What is daring analogy at one point is dangerous vagueness at another. So let us consider some character traits as intellectual virtues and vices. You need to figure out for yourself where you are on each scale. It is true, though, as Mr. Darcy says in *Pride and Prejudice*, that "[t]here is . . . in every disposition a tendency to some particular evil, a natural defect, which not even the best education can overcome." Each of us has at least one great weakness; understand it, and you come a long way toward controlling it.

Let us consider some important qualities of intellectual character. Take orderliness, for example. It is painfully obvious that orderliness is absolutely necessary for any major research project. A keen sense of research design, a mania about careful records and filing, a deliberate discipline of analysis—these are the avatars of orderliness necessary to undertake any major research enterprise, from an undergraduate paper to a multi-investigator project. But orderliness can also be important within thinking itself. It is very helpful to have an orderly mind. When you write out a big, long list of ideas, it's very useful to have the habit of rearranging the ideas every now and then into categories, changing the category system from time to time, to make it better and better. So in writing this chapter, I first wrote down dozens of free associations about judging ideas. Then I put them into a set of categories; there seemed to be some about talking to yourself, some about talking to others, and so on. Later (after adding some more ideas), I put those categories in an order for writing, figuring to move from the individual to the group and the literature and from the specific qualities to more general ones. Once I saw this emerging outline, I saw that I needed to split up one category and relabel a few others. I then sat down to write the chapter, creating categories *within* my headings (for example, the different types of personality qualities) and setting those in order as I came to write each section. This is a useful strategy for me, because I get worried when I've got a long list of somewhat related ideas but no clear structure for it.

Obviously, orderliness of thought is a good quality in mild doses. But as a dominating characteristic, it has problems. It is at the root of the reclassification papers mentioned earlier, papers whose only aim is to pull some idea or phenomenon out of one pigeonhole and put it into another. Pigeonholers also have a hard time finding phenomena *genuinely* puzzling. Their main concern is getting things into the proper boxes. Even worse, sometimes the pigeonholer has a personal, idiosyncratic set of boxes that other people don't have. Such pigeonholers often take things and deform them considerably to get them into classifiable shape. They can't leave things ambiguous and open. Yet this ability to leave things unresolved is absolutely necessary to a serious thinker.

Thus, orderliness is a quality that can cut both ways. So, too, is loyalty, in particular, loyalty to ideas. On the one hand, a certain loyalty to ideas is a great strength. Often a good idea doesn't show its colors for a while. It resists or evades. Loyalty to your ideas in the face of various kinds of criticisms is a strength. At the same time, it can become a liability. You have to know when to give up on ideas, when to set them aside and move on. Most of us have a little museum of cherished notions that have had to be rejected for this or that reason, much against our will. It's OK to keep these ideas in a personal museum, but they should probably stay there.

Another quality that cuts both ways is habit. There are many habits that are very useful. It is useful to have the habit of automatically verifying the logical structure of one's ideas before considering them further. It is useful to have the habit of listening to others as well as oneself. It is useful to know the conventions and usual disciplines of one's research area. At the same time, habit can become paralyzing. It can lead one to accept dead conventions. It can hide the paths of imagination completely.

Also two-faced is breadth of interest. There is something wonderful about a great breadth of interest, an ability to see the many things relevant to any given issue. Breadth of interest can open the doors to powerful analogies. It can bring distant methods to new uses. At the same time, excessive breadth (and depth) of interest can, like habit, be utterly paralyzing. In fact, the need to say everything one knows in every single paper is the most common single disease among young researchers. And excessive breadth of interest can lead to a variety of other pathologies: to pigeonholing, because only that can deal with such diverse interests; to arbitrary argument, because it will bring things together somehow; to sheer paralysis, because the range of topics is too great.

Related to breadth of interest is another quality with varying impact: imagination. It may seem odd at the end of a book aimed at increasing imagination to mention that it's possible to be too imaginative, but it is worth reflecting on imagination. There is more than a grain of truth in Edison's "genius is 99 percent perspiration and 1 percent inspiration." Ideas *do* need to be worked out. The working out is not easy. It is all too comfortable to avoid recasting one's ideas because "others don't see the imaginative links I have made," and so on. Most of the time when your ideas don't survive the tests presented earlier in this chapter, they're bad ideas. If they don't sustain—indeed, call out for—careful elaboration, they're probably just flimsy analogies with nothing in them. So watch out for congratulating yourself on your imagination. It can be a cover-up for flimsy thinking.

There is also an underlying personality difference at issue here. Some people have a tendency to see things as alike (by making analogies); others see things as different (by making distinctions). Many years ago, the personnel directors of Bell Laboratories found these tendencies to be so strong that they tried to make sure that S (similarities) engineers worked for S bosses and D (differences) engineers for D bosses. This quality of seeing similarities or seeing differences is captured in the old mathematics joke that a topologist is a mathematician who can't tell a doughnut from a coffee cup. (A doughnut and a coffee cup are topologically equivalent, since a plane intersecting them can intersect two disconnected parts, something that can't happen with a pencil or a tennis ball, which are topologically equivalent to each other but not to doughnuts or coffee cups.) Topologists are *very* abstract mathematicians. Things that look utterly different to the rest of us look alike to them.[1]

As the Bell Labs reference makes clear, this quality of seeing similarities or differences takes on much of its color relationally, from the habits of others around you. To be an S person in the midst of a group of Ds can mean that you're treated as a visionary or a visionary crank. To be a D in a group of Ss can define you as a plodding pigeonholer or as someone with his or her feet on the ground. It is worth trying to figure out your general habit. Do you look for similarities? build down from abstractions? make strong assumptions? Or do you see differences? build up inductively? keep all the details straight? As with so many qualities, it is best to alternate between these styles if you can.

We come now to the more publicly evident qualities of an intellectual personality. Of these, by far the most important is self-confidence. In general, everyone in academia thinks he or she can judge the self-confidence of others by noting how much they talk. In fact, there's much else involved in talking too much. People can talk a lot because they know a lot or because they come from talky cultures or because they are trying to persuade themselves that they have something to say or, in some cases, simply because they are arrogant.

There is probably nothing more important than coming to a good sense of your own degree of self-confidence. It's pretty easy to tell if you have too much self-confidence. If you can't quickly think of two or three people who have recently taught you something important about a topic you thought you knew well, you are probably too self-confident. If you do most of the talking in most of your classes or in groups of friends, you are probably too self-confident. If you don't have to rewrite most of your papers three or four times, you are probably too self-confident. If you can't take criticism, you are probably too self-confident. Generally, overconfident students are unaware of their overconfidence. If they do recognize their tendency to domineer, they may put it down to other things: educational advantage, prior study, desire to help others, and so on. By contrast, students who lack self-confidence are usually quite aware of their timidity, but they often do not see it as their problem so much as that of other students, who (they think) domineer.

In an odd way, people who have too much self-confidence have much the same problem as people who have too little.

Neither one gets the feedback necessary to learn from others. People with too much self-confidence don't pay attention to what others have to say, even if they give them time to say it. They therefore lose most of what other people have to tell them. This makes their own intellectual development harder. They are only as good as their own ability to judge and improve their ideas. They don't find out about facts that others happen to have noticed. They don't hear that others have tried out certain intellectual paths and found them useless. It's as if Mark Granovetter's job seekers (in Chapter Four) were trying to find jobs on their own, without all the weak ties—you can do it, but it takes a long time. The short-run reward for such people is always being right. But the long-run costs are great. They deny themselves the help others can give. Only truly outstanding talent can make much headway with such a handicap, and even then only at the price of incredible labor.

People who lack self-confidence also lose what others have to tell them, but not because they don't listen. Rather, they listen too much, never risking their own ideas independently. As a result, they often end up following the lead of something outside themselves—a book, a friend, a teacher—and never really learn to think for themselves. They can do well under certain academic conditions—particularly if they are students of an overconfident teacher, but they cannot learn to think on their own because they do not risk their own ideas.

Finally, a few words about the emotions of ideas. Having good ideas can be an emotional business. You need to recognize when those emotions take over. For those of us who analogize (as I do, for example), there are moments when we get into an analogizing mood and everything in the world looks like markets or networks or nested dichotomies or whatever our fascination is for the moment. It's like falling in love. Everything you read seems to fit the analogy perfectly, just as everything about the person you fall in love with seems to fit perfectly with your interests and desires. Feelings can be just as strong for other styles of intellectual personality. The pigeonholer can ponder, with sweet indecision, which might be the best of four or five ways of viewing patrimonial bureaucracies, all the while speculating on the many details one might use to place them better as a type of administration or, perhaps better still, to break them down into patrimonial bureaucracies set up as such and patrimonial bureaucracies deriving from the gradual breakdown of rules in meritocratic administrative systems. Every intellectual personality has its moods of excitement, when hard work becomes pleasure and Edison's 99 percent perspiration suddenly disappears into the 1 percent genius.

As in love, so here, too, it is worth surrendering yourself to the excitement for a while, maybe for a good, long while. Indulge yourself. Wallow in your ideas. But remember that ultimately ideas are for communicating to others, so you have to stand back and judge them, just as you have to stand back and decide whether to move in with or marry someone you love. An idea you become serious about is just like somebody you live with. You get familiar with it. You use it daily. You see it wearing a bathrobe and slippers, without its makeup or aftershave. But you should feel you can never come to the end of it, that it retains the sudden enticement and novelty that grabbed you to begin with, that it continues to challenge and provoke. You shouldn't move in with an idea that doesn't have that kind of endless power and excitement.

The love metaphor suggests something else important. Remember that you and your idea need to spend time alone, without distraction. That means no music, no TV, no talking roommates. Do what you must to create a private world in which you can get to know your idea in depth. For me, it means (I confess it) walking around and talking aloud to an invisible companion about my idea. (My invisible companion doesn't mind when I say things twice or resay them or get boring or whatever, which is very useful.) Somehow, talking my ideas through to someone imaginary makes me more conscious of how others will hear them. (Of course, it's also great fun; an imaginary listener always knows just how far to push you and when to shut up.)

You will do something different, no doubt: perhaps sit in a certain place and look at certain scenery, perhaps clear your mind with certain music before sitting down to think, perhaps take a long walk. The point is that ideas—like the social reality I discussed in the opening pages of this book—have to be wooed to be won. They don't just show up fully dressed and ready to step out for a lovely evening on the town. And they want your full attention, not part of it.

VI. PUZZLES

All of this brings us to my final topic: the question of puzzles. In the very beginning, I suggested that one of the odd qualities of social science is that we often start a project with only a relatively general interest in an area. Finding the real puzzle and finding its solution occur together as we go forward. I now need to clarify that idea.

What does it mean to say that we start out with a general interest and aren't clear at first what our puzzle is? Consider the rare reverse case: once in a while, a research project starts with a striking, clear, puzzling fact. I once noticed that status rankings of professionals within professions were different from status rankings of professionals by those outside. Professionals themselves give highest respect to colleagues who have little to do with clients: consulting physicians, lawyer team leaders, elite researchers. The public, by contrast, gives highest respect to front-line, hardworking professionals in the thick of client problems: primary-case physicians, courtroom attorneys, classroom teachers. Why should this be? I was working on the psychiatric profession at the time, and this empirical puzzle simply occurred to me one morning while I was thinking about the fact that high-status psychiatrists talked to upper-middle-class clients with minimal difficulties while low-status psychiatrists worked in mental hospitals with mostly lower-class clients with huge difficulties, as I and most people then imagined most psychiatrists did. It was one of those rare occasions when there is an obvious empirical puzzle and a straight march of the research from puzzle to solution.

Most of the time, however, clear puzzles don't appear in data. We are more likely to start out by playing at normal science with our data, trying out all the old additive tricks: What is the effect of another variable? Does such and such a finding hold up in another setting? At the same time, we are generally being urged on by the general (and insoluble) problems that probably got us into social science in the first place: Why does society have the statuses that it has? How does real social change occur? What drives the division of labor? How are prices and values established? Interesting as these problems are, they are nearly devoid of real content. We can't directly reason about them because the very words in them have infinitely contestable meanings. Status, social change, division of labor, price, value—none of these has a fixed, context-free meaning.

So most often, we find ourselves with a general concern of this type, a mass of data that we can see as relevant to that general interest, and a hunch that bringing the concern and the data together will lead us to a more specific puzzle and a solution. The real issue is how we recognize a puzzle in this amorphous confrontation between interest and data.

Like coming up with ideas, finding things puzzling is very much a matter of taste and knowledge. The knowledge part is obvious. You can't tell whether something is puzzling unless you expect it to be different from what it is. That expectation rests on what you already know. So the basis for finding things surprising is knowing about things that aren't surprising. This is why undergraduate majors require survey courses and why graduate programs (ought to) have general examinations. You have to know the background before you can see that something doesn't fit into it. Note that this explains why people who write pure social theory never come up with much. If you don't know anything about the world, it's hard to see what parts of the world call out for explanation. You end up writing theories of theories.

But there is an issue of taste involved as well. Seeing things as puzzles means being willing to live with ambiguity. If your first instinct with any unusual fact is to jam it into a category or to rationalize it in terms of your favorite idea, you are going to have trouble seeing puzzles. Our minds are powerful ratio-nalizers, and seeing puzzles means, in part, shutting down that powerful pattern-making machine or, more precisely, letting it drift a bit. Note that this is another place where excessive self-confidence gets in the way. Self-confident people, particularly of the arrogant variety, aren't happy running the engine on idle for a bit. But that idling often helps in seeing puzzles; *not* having the instant answer is what leads to success.

Some of us rely on external puzzle generators. Thus, for many social scientists, puzzle recognition originates in political or moral commitments. The 1960s was a time of strong politi-cal and moral commitments—of many different kinds—and those who entered social science in that period usually had a sense that inequality, war, social change, and so on, were burn-ing concerns. No matter what the particular direction of their commitments, these people came to social science already thinking that these phenomena were deeply interesting. They might have thought inequality was wrong, or they might have been angry with people who thought inequality was wrong, but they all thought inequality was extremely important and in many ways puzzling.

The danger of the moral-political source for puzzles is that one always sees the same puzzle. The result is what one of my female colleagues dismisses as "research of the form 'add women and stir.' " Such research is not terribly interesting be-cause it soon becomes relentless normal science. The moral-political source for puzzles works only if one allows new puzzles to grow perpetually within one's broader concern. So you can start with the puzzle of explaining why women and men seem so often to behave differently but then go on to worry about why it is that within women's groups we often see repeated many of the patterns of difference that we see between the sexes. These subpuzzles can often be in tension with the original driving puzzle, however, and so tend to force a choice to either stick with the original puzzle or allow the subpuzzles to take on a logic of their own. Among the best of the politically-morally motivated, it is precisely the tension between these two logics that drives their creativity.

For some people—this is more characteristic of generations after the 1960s—the social world is perplexing because they are perplexed by their own position in it. The most common form of this attitude today manifests itself in what we usually call identity research. This is research motivated by and focused on some particular identity or attribute of the researcher: gender, ethnicity, race, or whatever. Often identity research takes the form of "Is there any sorrow like my sorrow?" in which case we have the strengths and weaknesses of the political-moral puzzles I just mentioned. The strength is strength of commitment and depth of interest. The weakness is the danger of bias and relentlessly unimaginative normal science.

One can also be driven to study divorce or disability or schooling or wealth because of immediate personal experiences that may not be identity related. If you talk with faculty members at any length, you will find a surprising number whose motivations are of this kind. It is sobering that usually these "experience-motivated" faculty members are reacting to unhappy experiences. Tolstoy was right when he said that "all happy families are alike, but an unhappy family is unhappy after its own fashion." To judge by social science practice, there is something quite uninteresting about positive experiences. Little is written about them, although a school of "well-being" research has finally taken root on the frontiers of psychology and economics.

The most important weakness of these personal motivations is not one from which students suffer. It is, rather, a problem for middle-aged faculty. If we figure out our basic puzzle, we don't have a new source for problems. Perhaps it is this that explains the surprising number of social scientists who undertake passionate research as young professionals and then go to sleep intellectually in middle age, as their personal problems loom smaller in a life filled with marriage, children, students, hobbies, professional and institutional eminence, and so on.

There are, then, personal sources for puzzles as well as social ones. All of these various sources can be dangerous because they give us particular desires for particular kinds of results, because they can get mindlessly routine, and because they are good only as long as the personal and social concerns last. But they also can provide an energy and passion that drive our need to understand a puzzling world. These are the driving forces behind most great social scientists.

There are those, finally, who simply find the social world intrinsically interesting and puzzling, just as some of us wanted to know all about snakes or tadpoles as little kids. Lucky people. And to be blunt, very rare people. For every person whose passion for social science comes from truly disinterested curiosity, there are dozens whose passion arose originally from personal and social concerns. Faculty who are deeply puzzled about the social world without having a personal or social agenda are often the hardest to come to know. Their passionately disinterested curiosity seems strange to the majority of us, who have come to social science from personal and social concerns. But they are always among the most creative.

A rich vein of puzzlement is then something that all good social scientists have, whether they are beginning undergraduates, graduate students, or senior professors. Whatever its source, this puzzlement becomes a compulsion to figure out the nature of social life. When you find faculty who have it, learn from them. They will have their faults, often great ones, but they have much to teach and are themselves willing to learn. These are the people who will help you find your own gifts of sociological imagination.

Bear in mind, however, that there are active and even talented social scientists who *don't* have this creative puzzlement. These are faculty members who do social science not for love but for a living, going through conventional motions often with considerable success, a success they value more highly than inquiry itself. You will recognize them by their behavior: one is smart but condescending and uninterested; another is eminent but conventional and stale. When you go to office hours and meet such people or their cousin the bland, busy professional with all the answers but no ideas, extricate yourself graciously. Such people have nothing to teach you.

Above all, what they lack is imagination. I said at the outset that social science is a conversation between rigor and imagination. Just as rigor can be practiced and mastered, so can imagination be developed and cherished. I hope in this book to have suggested some useful exercises for doing that. But I have only suggested. It is now for you to find the excitement that comes with inventing your own heuristics and reimagining the social world.

GLOSSARY

additive heuristic. The heuristic move of doing more of the same: finding more data, making a new dimension of analysis, making use of a new methodological wrinkle.

argument heuristic. The heuristic move that turns a familiar argument into a completely new one. The main argument heuristics are problematizing the obvious, reversal, making or denying radical assumptions, and reconceptualizing.

behaviorism. The position that one cannot measure (or study) the meanings that actors assign to action. One can study only behavior: external actions that are measurable in a reliable and replicable manner. *Opposed to* **culturalism.**

case study. A study of a single, particular social actor, object, or situation.

causality. The reasons things occur. Causality was thought by Aristotle to come in four brands (material, formal, proximate, and final) and by Hume to be unknowable (we can know only regular patterns, not their causes). It is a shibboleth of **standard causal analysis.**

cluster analysis. A quantitative technique that sorts objects into groups based on information about resemblance or distance between the objects. *See also* **data-reduction techniques.**

conflict/consensus. The debate over whether disorder in social life results from disorderly and oppressive institutions (conflict theory) or from insufficient regulation of inherently disorderly individuals (consensus theory).

constructionism. The position that the things and the qualities of things encountered in social reality are continuously reproduced anew in interaction. *Opposed to* **realism.**

contextualism. The belief that social facts make no sense when abstracted from the other social facts that surround them in social time and space.

correlational analysis. A form of quantitative analysis based on the study of the covariation of variables.

culturalism. The position that the symbolic systems of culture can and must be studied. *Opposed to* **behaviorism.**

culture. The symbolic systems by which social actors understand, experience, and direct their lives.

data-reduction techniques. Any of a number of techniques for turning complex data into simpler data, by reducing them either to groupings (cluster analysis) or to simpler dimensions. The latter can be based on intercase distance (multidimensional scaling) or direct reduction of the variables (factor analysis).

descriptive heuristic. The heuristic move that radically changes the way we describe some aspect of social reality. The important descriptive gambits are changing the context, changing levels, and lumping and splitting.

emergent. A real social phenomenon that extends beyond a single individual. The existence of emergents is denied by **methodological individualism.**

ethnography. A method of analyzing social life through participation of varying degrees in the situation analyzed.

explanation. A satisfactory account of a phenomenon. *For specific types, see* **pragmatic explanation; semantic explanation; syntactic explanation.**

explanatory program. A broad class of methods aimed at a particular general strategy or type of explanation. Hence, for example, *syntactic explanatory program* denotes methods aiming at excellence in syntactic explanation.

factor analysis. A data-reduction technique based on modeling quantitative data in reduced dimensions (classical-factor model) or on an iterative search for the simplest dimensions that will "contain" all the quantitative information (principal-components analysis). *See also* **data-reduction techniques.**

formalization. A general name for those methods aiming at highly formalized analysis of social life, usually without the use of data other than stylized facts.

fractal debates. Basic disagreements about issues of method or conception in social science, all of which have the fractal property of recurring at finer and finer levels, always in the same form.

fractal heuristic. The heuristic move that operates by using one of the classic debates of social science to open a new space for analysis.

game theory. A type of formalization that models social reality as a game among some number of players subject to various rules and payoff patterns. There are hundreds of possible games: Prisoners' Dilemma, Tit for Tat, and so on.

general linear model (GLM). A general mathematical model for data in which the dependent variable is a linear function of the independent variables plus some error terms. On certain assumptions, the parameters of this model can be estimated. The vast majority of quantitative social science uses some version of GLM, either directly or after the transformation of variables from nonlinear to linear forms.

grand narrative. A narrative of large-scale social actors over substantial time periods, usually glossing over details for subgroups, subproblems, and so on.

heuristic. A discipline that aims to facilitate invention and discovery of new facts and ideas in the sciences.

historical narration. A method of analyzing social life by telling stories based on the extensive reading of primary documents.

interaction effect. In linear models for data, an effect that involves combinations of variables, such that variable X's effect on variable Z depends on the level of variable Y or vice versa. These can be of varying types: multiplicative effects, suppressor effects, curvilinear effects, and so on. They create serious problems for nearly all types of estimation and interpretation of coefficients. Opposed to *main effects*, the effects of independent variables when taken singly.

interpretivism. The position that social facts cannot be measured without taking account of their meaning, usually for a particular actor, time, and place. *Opposed to* **positivism.**

literary structuralism. A movement, dating largely from the 1960s and 1970s, advocating the formal analysis of literary texts.

metacritique. The critique of one method by another based on the application of the critiquing method to the practices of the critiqued method.

method. A set of standard procedures and assumptions for carrying out some form of rigorous social analysis.

methodological individualism. The position that all social phenomena are merely apparent and have no "reality" beyond that of the individuals who are held to generate them. See also **emergent; reduction.**

methodology. The discipline of investigating methods. The word is also often used as an equivalent of *method*, as in the phrase "What is your methodology?" meaning "What method did you use?"

microeconomics. The branch of economics concerned with the behavior of multitudes of identical actors in simple markets under simple constraints; founded on concepts of the relationships among supply, demand, price, and budget constraint.

model. In quantitative social science, the mathematical form relating variables to one another. Typically, the relationships involve scalar coefficients (also known as parameters), which must be estimated by some mathematical function of the data.

multidimensional scaling. A quantitative technique that turns information about resemblance or distance between a set of social objects into a map of the objects (usually in two or three dimensions), retaining in the map as much of the original distance information as possible. See also **data-reduction techniques.**

multiple regression. An alternative name for the standard linear model for independent and dependent variables, not to be confused with ordinary least squares (OLS), generalized least squares (GLS), maximum-likelihood estimation (MLE), and so on, which are names for different sets of assumptions (and the algorithms associated with those assumptions) that are used to estimate the parameters of these (and other) models.

narrative heuristic. The heuristic move that works by changing the way we use stories and events to describe the social process. The important narrative heuristics are putting something into motion or stopping it, changing the role we assign to contingency, considering latent functions, and examining counterfactuals.

network analysis. A formal method emphasizing investigation of the patterns of connections between actors, groups, or institutions and the consequences of those patterns. Originally highly formalistic but increasingly married to causal methods.

normal science. Kuhn's term for science that is cumulative and routine, accepting the basic methods, assumptions, and concepts of a paradigm. *See also* **paradigm.**

paradigm. Kuhn's term for the set of methods, assumptions, and concepts that make possible a type of normal science. Change in paradigm constitutes scientific revolution. *See also* **normal science.**

path analysis. In quantitative analysis, a way of combining multiple regressions on certain assumptions to present "path coefficients" in a network diagram in order to represent the causal effects of a set of variables on one another in sequence.

positivism. The position that social facts can be reliably measured and that such measurement need not take account of their meaning for particular actors. *Opposed to* **interpretivism.**

pragmatic explanation. Explanation that is designed to facilitate action and is hence strongly aimed at necessary causes.

rational choice. A name loosely applied to methods employing economic theories of choice as models for noneconomic types of human behavior.

realism. The position that the things and qualities of things encountered in social reality are more or less given and stable, rather than continuously reproduced in interaction. *Opposed to* **constructionism.**

reduction. An explanation that works by translating "higher-level" phenomena to "lower-level" ones. *See also* **methodological individualism,** which is usually regarded as a form of reduction.

search heuristic. The heuristic move of getting new ideas from outside the areas customarily used for them in the type of research being done. The two basic search heuristics are making an analogy and borrowing a method.

semantic explanation. An explanation that works by translating unexplained phenomena into familiar phenomena that we understand commonsensically.

simulation. A type of formalization based on iteration of some simple system of rules or patterns designed to capture the behavior of a set of actors. *See also* **formalization.**

small-N analysis. A general name for analysis of a relatively small number of cases in greater detail than standard causal analysis allows. Small-N analysis typically involves from two or three to a few dozen cases and often uses a variety of methods. *See also* **standard causal analysis.**

social structure. Regular and routine patterns of behavior of whatever size or extent.

standard causal analysis (SCA). A general name for quantitative methods based on treating independent variables as representing causes of social phenomena. SCA includes both general-linear-model analysis and survival analysis. *See also* causality; general linear model; variable, dependent; variables, independent.

structural equation. A quantitative model that allows reciprocal causation and hence does away with the distinction between dependent and independent variables. Structural equations are difficult to estimate and involve very strong assumptions.

stylized fact. A simplified, highly abstract form of data designed to capture general patterns in a variable or parameter without actually measuring it.

survey method. The gathering of data via the administration of questionnaires or other uniform instruments to a selected sample of respondents.

survival method. A quantitative method in which the dependent variable is the time until some event occurs. Also called *durational method*.

syntactic explanation. An explanation in which the formal perfection (or elegance, beauty, generality, or some other quality) of the explanation is emphasized.

time-series method. A method based on models of successive values of a variable or variables. In economics, time-series methods are most commonly done on dozens of time periods but only one variable. In sociology, they are more often done on few time intervals but with many variables, with the data from the different time intervals typically pooled.

variable, dependent. In standard causal analysis, the variable that is predicted by all the others. *See also* **standard causal analysis.**

variables, independent. In standard causal analysis, the set of variables used to predict values of another, dependent variable. *See also* **standard causal analysis.**

NOTES

CHAPTER 1   EXPLANATION

1. As the great anthropologist Evans-Pritchard once remarked,

> Anyone who is not a complete idiot can do fieldwork, and if the people he is working among have not been studied before he cannot help making an original contribution to knowledge. . . . Anyone can produce a new fact; the thing is to produce a new idea." (1976:243)

In the more theoretical phraseology of Imre Lakatos (1970:132ff.), the most important quality of research programs is their "heuristic power," their ability to keep producing new ideas and point the way to new findings.

2. Among many writers who have made the case for "beauty" in scientific argument, see Chandrasekhar (1979).

3. Syntactics, semantics, and pragmatics are the three fundamental aspects of all systems of signs, of which explanation is an example. See Morris (1938).

4. The words for denoting methods are changing. Properly speaking, a method is a set of routine procedures for rigorous inquiry. Methodology is (literally) discussion of methods. Ethnography or standard causal analysis (SCA), then, is a method, while to write *about* ethnography or SCA is to write methodology. In practice, people are now often using *methodology* to mean "method," as in the familiar seminar question, "What's your methodology?" Note that people using these terms do not customarily use *methodical* as the adjective form of *method*; they use *methodological*, which is thus the adjective form used for *both* *method* and *methodology*. I have tried to maintain the traditional distinction between method and methodology throughout.

5. Sometimes quantitative analysts do undertake detailed study of several cases. For an example, see Paige (1975).

6. Of course, when we look at the facts, the situation is much more drastic. Black and white tolerances are by no means as auspicious as the Schelling models presume. It is, then, hardly surprising that American neighborhoods stably integrated at any ratio beyond 20 percent black are extremely rare.

7. One should not necessarily think that one or the other of these has priority as a mode of thinking even about causality. If we consider the literature on causality, there have been distinguished exponents both of the idea that causality must involve passage of time and of the idea that it *cannot* involve passage of time. See Abbott (2001b:c. 3).

8. To save space, I do not comment in depth on the temporal versions of the SCA program. But in fact, the same discussion governs them. To be sure, they are embedded in time and because of that acquire a semantic verisimilitude that cross-sectional studies lack. But they still function on the semantic level of variables, far removed from narrative understandings of the unfolding of events. Durational methods can predict "particular" events, like the passing of a law or the founding of a newspaper, but they do so with the same kinds of disembodied variables (rather than complex particulars) that are used by cross-sectional methods. So they remain at a considerable semantic distance from immediately familiar worlds.

CHAPTER 2   BASIC DEBATES AND METHODOLOGICAL PRACTICES

1. Or that people's frames of reference are distributed independently of those things about them that we are trying to investigate. In that case, we can treat the errors that arise in their answers as noise. Of course, the problem is that we don't know whether the frames of reference are correlated with things we want to investigate, and we can't answer that question without new data.

2. "Narrative positivism" is a move discussed in Abbott (2001b:c. 6).

CHAPTER 3   INTRODUCTION TO HEURISTICS

1. The conventionally correct pronunciation of εύρηκα according to Anglophone classicists is HEH-oo-ray-ka, not the popular culture's you-REE-ka. In fact, nobody really knows how ancient Greek was pronounced.

2. There is not yet a clear usage defining the difference between *heuristic* and *heuristics*. It is agreed that *heuristic* is the adjective, as in "a heuristic inquiry." But for the noun, things are unclear. Pólya used *heuristic* to denote the discipline of discovery generally but had no shorthand word for a single heuristic move, nor any plural for a collection of several such moves (1957). Many writers now speak of a heuristic when referring to a particular heuristic rule ("the analogy heuristic," and so on). This is the usual usage in computer science.

There, *heuristics* serves as the simple plural for the singular *heuristic*. I shall try to follow both of these usages here, in parallel with the standard usage of *logic*. One speaks of logic as the discipline, modal or formal logic as individual logic systems, and logics as collections of several such logic systems. So here with heuristic(s).

CHAPTER 4   GENERAL HEURISTICS: SEARCH AND ARGUMENT HEURISTICS

1. My first sociological statement of this borrowing was in Abbott and Hrycak (1990). For a general review of the "mini-industry," see Abbott and Tsay (2000).

CHAPTER 6   FRACTAL HEURISTICS

1. This argument led eventually to a joke about a Chicago economist and his student walking down the road. The student tells his mentor he sees a one-hundred-dollar bill on the ground. The economist says, "You should have your eyes examined. If a bill were there, someone would have picked it up."

2. Desrosières and Thévenot (1988); Szreter (1984); Conk [Anderson] (1980).

CHAPTER 7   IDEAS AND PUZZLES

1. I was referred to the discussion of scientists at Bell Labs many years ago by my father, who, I think, correctly saw in these ideas the reason why he and I had such a hard time talking about mathematics and other technical subjects: he loved the distinctions; I loved the similarities. I didn't get the point that he was talking about him and me—rather than some abstract issue—until many years later. In this particular case, he saw the similarity and I didn't. Moreover, when I showed him this note, he told me he thought of himself as a similarities person as well. So he saw yet another similarity that I did not.

REFERENCES

Abbott, A. 1988. *The System of Professions*. Chicago: University of Chicago Press.

———. 1995. "Things of Boundaries." *Social Research* 62:857–82.

———. 2001a. *Chaos of Disciplines*. Chicago: University of Chicago Press.

———. 2001b. *Time Matters*. Chicago: University of Chicago Press.

Abbott, A., and A. Hrycak. 1990. "Measuring Resemblance in Social Sequences." *American Journal of Sociology* 96:144–85.

———, and A. Tsay. 2000. "Sequence Analysis and Optimal Matching Methods in Sociology." *Sociological Methods and Research* 29:3–33.

Abell, P. 1987. *The Syntax of Social Life*. Oxford and New York: Clarendon Press.

———. 1990. "Games in Networks." *Rationality and Society* 1:259–82.

Ainslie, G. 1992. *Picoeconomics*. Cambridge: Cambridge University Press.

Allenbrook, W. J. 1983. *Rhythmic Gesture in Mozart*. Chicago: University of Chicago Press.

Barth, F. 1966. *Models of Social Organization*. Occasional Paper, no. 23. London: Royal Anthropological Institute.

Beck, E. M., P. M. Horan, and C. M Tolbert II. 1978. "Stratification in a Dual Economy." *American Sociological Review* 43:704–20.

Becker, G. 1957. *The Economics of Discrimination*. Chicago: University of Chicago Press.

Becker, H. S. 1962. "Becoming a Marihuana User." In *Outsiders*, 41–58. New York: Free Press.

Berk, R. A., and S. F. Berk. 1978. "A Simultaneous Equation Model for the Division of Household Labor." *Sociological Methods and Research* 6:431–68.

Blau, P., and O. D. Duncan. 1967. *The American Occupational Structure*. New York: Free Press.

Bott, E. 1955. "Urban Families." *Human Relations* 8:345–84.

Bourdieu, P. 1984. *Distinction*. Cambridge, Mass.: Harvard University Press.

Braudel, F. [1949] 1972–73. *The Mediterranean and the Mediterranean World in the Age of Phillip II*. Trans. Siân Reynolds. 2 vols. New York: Harper and Row.

Burawoy, M. 1979. *Manufacturing Consent*. Chicago: University of Chicago Press.

Burke, K. 1969. *A Grammar of Motives*. Berkeley: University of California Press.

Burt, R. S. 1983. "Cohesion versus Structural Equivalence as a Basis for Network Subgroups." In *Applied Network Analysis*, ed. R. S. Burt and M. J. Minor, 262–82. Beverly Hills, Calif.: Sage Publications.

Carlin, J. 1962. *Lawyers on Their Own*. New Brunswick, N.J.: Rutgers University Press.

Chambliss, D. F. 1989. "The Mundanity of Excellence." *Sociological Theory* 7:70–86.

———. 1992. "Reply to DeNora's Comment." *Sociological Theory* 10:103–05.

Chandrasekhar, S. 1979. "Beauty and the Quest for Beauty in Science." *Physics Today* 32:25–30.

Clarke, M. L. [1953] 1996. *Rhetoric at Rome*. Revised by D. H. Berry. London: Routledge.

Coase, R. 1937. "The Nature of the Firm." *Economica* 4:386–405.

Cohen, L. C., and M. Felson. 1979. "Social Change and Crime Trends." *American Sociological Review* 44:588–608.

Cole, D. 1985. *Captured Heritage*. Vancouver: University of British Columbia Press.

Cole, D., and I. Chaikin. 1990. *An Iron Hand upon the People*. Vancouver: Douglas and McIntyre.

Collingwood, R. G. 1946. *The Idea of History*. Oxford: Oxford University Press.

Conk, M. A. 1980. *The United States Census and Labor Force Change*. Ann Arbor, Mich.: UMI Research Press.

DeNora, T. 1992. "Comment on Chambliss's 'The Mundanity of Excellence.' " *Sociological Theory* 10:99–102.

Desrosières, A., and L. Thévenot. 1988. *Les catégories socioprofessionelles*. Paris: Éditions La Découverte.

Dewey, J. [1916] 1966. *Democracy and Education*. New York: Free Press.

DiMaggio, P. J., and W. W. Powell. 1983. "The Iron Cage Revisited." *American Sociological Review* 48:147–60.

Douglas, M. 1966. *Purity and Danger*. London: Routledge and Kegan Paul.

Duesenberry, J. 1960. "Comment" in *Demography and Economic Change in Developed Countries*, 231–40. Princeton, N.J.: Princeton University Press.

Duneier, M. 1999. *Sidewalk*. New York: Farrar, Strauss and Giroux.

Durkheim, E. 1897. *Suicide*. Paris: Alcan.

Edwards, R. 1979. *Contested Terrain*. New York: Basic Books.

Elias, N. [1939] 1994. *The Civilizing Process*. Trans. E. Jephcott. Oxford and Cambridge, Mass.: Blackwell.

Epstein, C. F. 1983. *Women in Law*. Garden City, N.Y.: Doubleday.

Evans-Pritchard, E. E. [1937] 1976. *Withcraft, Oracles, and Magic among the Azande*. Abridged Ed. Oxford: Clarendon Press.

Farkas, G. 1976. "Education, Wage Rates, and the Division of Labor between Husband and Wife." *Journal of Marriage and the Family* 38:473–83.

Fischer, C. 1982. *To Dwell among Friends*. Chicago: University of Chicago Press.

Fleck, L. [1935] 1979. *The Genesis and Development of a Scientific Fact.* Chicago: University of Chicago Press.

Fogel, R. W. 1964. *Railroads and American Economic Growth.* Baltimore: Johns Hopkins University Press.

Fogel, R. W., and S. Engerman. 1974. *Time on the Cross.* 2 vols. Boston: Little, Brown.

Forrester, J. W. 1961. *Industrial Dynamics.* Cambridge, Mass.: MIT Press.

———. 1969. *Urban Dynamics.* Cambridge, Mass.: MIT Press.

———. 1971. *World Dynamics.* Cambridge, Mass.: Wright Allen Press.

Gallie, W. B. 1968. *Philosophy and the Historical Understanding.* New York: Schocken Books.

Geertz, C. 1973. "Thick Description." In *The Interpretation of Cultures*, 3–30. New York: Basic Books.

Goffman, E. 1959. *The Presentation of Self in Everyday Life.* Garden City, N.Y.: Doubleday.

Granovetter, M. 1973. "The Strength of Weak Ties." *American Journal of Sociology* 78:1360–80.

———. 1974. *Getting a Job.* Cambridge, Mass.: Harvard University Press.

Gusfield, J. 1981. *The Culture of Public Problems.* Chicago: University of Chicago Press.

Haggett, P., A. Cliff, and A. Frey. 1977. *Locational Analysis in Human Geography.* New York: John Wiley.

Hannan, M. T., and J. Freeman. 1977. "The Population Ecology of Organizations." *American Journal of Sociology* 82:929–64.

Hempel, C. G. 1942. "The Function of General Laws in History." *Journal of Philosophy* 39:35–48.

Hirschi, T., and M. Gottfredson. 1983. "Age and the Explanation of Crime." *American Journal of Sociology* 89:552–84.

Hochschild, A. 1983. *The Managed Heart.* Berkeley: University of California Press.

Hodge, R. W., P. M. Siegel, and P. H. Rossi. 1966. "Occupational Prestige in the United States, 1925–1963." In *Class, Status and Power*, 2d ed., edited by R. Bendix and S. M. Lipset, 322–34. New York: Free Press.

Holmes, T. H., and R. H. Rahe. 1967. "The Social Readjustment Rating Scale." *Journal of Psychosomatic Research* 11:213–18.

Kahneman, D., and A. Tversky. 1979. "Prospect Theory." *Econometrica* 47:263–92.

Kessler, R. C., R. H. Price, and C. B. Wortman. 1985. "Social Factors in Psychopathology." *Annual Review of Psychology* 36:531–72.

Key, V. O. 1955. "A Theory of Critical Elections." *Journal of Politics* 17:3–18.

Kuhn, T. [1962] 1970. *The Structure of Scientific Revolutions.* Chicago: University of Chicago Press.

Kuklinski, J. H., E. Riggle, V. Ottati, N. Schwartz, and R. S. Wyer. 1991. "The Cognitive and Affective Bases of Political Tolerance Judgments." *American Journal of Political Science* 35:1–27.

Lakatos, I. 1970. "Falsification and the Methodology of Scientific Research Programmes."

In *Criticism and the Growth of Knowledge,* edited by I. Lakatos and A. Musgrave, 91–196. Cambridge: Cambridge University Press.

Latour, B., and S. Woolgar. 1979. *Laboratory Life.* Beverly Hills, Calif.: Sage Publications.

Laumann, E. O., and D. Knoke. 1987. *The Organizational State.* Madison: University of Wisconsin Press.

Leach, Edmund. [1954] 1964. *Political Systems of Highland Burma.* Boston: Beacon Press.

Le Roy Ladurie, E. 1978. *Montaillou.* Trans. B. Bray. New York: George Braziller.

Lesthaeghe, R. 1983. "A Century of Demographic and Cultural Change in Western Europe." *Population and Development Review* 9:411–35.

Lévi-Strauss, C. 1967. "The Structural Study of Myth." In *Structural Anthropology,* 202–38. Garden City, N.Y.: Doubleday.

Lieberson, S. 1985. *Making It Count.* Berkeley: University of California Press.

Lorrain, F., and H. C. White. 1971. "Structural Equivalence of Individuals in Social Networks." *Journal of Mathematical Sociology* 1:49–80.

Malinowski, B. [1922] 1961. *Argonauts of the Western Pacific.* New York: E. P. Dutton.

———. [1967] 1989. *A Diary in the Strict Sense of the Term.* Stanford, Calif.: Stanford University Press.

Mandeville, B. [1714, 1729] 1957. *The Fable of the Bees.* Oxford: Clarendon Press.

Mayhew, P., R. Clarke, and D. Eliot. 1989. "Motorcycle Theft, Helmet Registration, and Displacement." *Howard Journal of Criminal Justice* 28:1–8.

Meyer, J. W., and B. Rowan. 1977. "Institutionalized Organizations." *American Journal of Sociology* 83:340–63.

Mills, J. 1946. *The Engineer in Society.* New York: Van Nostrand.

Mintz, S. 1985. *Sweetness and Power.* New York: Viking Press.

Mirowski, P. 1989. *More Heat Than Light.* Cambridge: Cambridge University Press.

Mohr, J., and V. Duquenne. 1997. "The Duality of Culture and Practice." *Theory and Society* 26:305–56.

Moore, B. 1966. *The Social Origins of Dictatorship and Democracy.* Boston: Beacon Press.

Morris, C. 1938. *Foundations of the Theory of Signs.* Vol. 1, no. 2, of *International Encyclopedia of the Unity of Science,* ed. O. Neurath. Chicago: University of Chicago Press.

Muth, J. F. 1961. "Rational Expectations and the Theory of Price Movements." *Econometrica* 29:315–35.

Nader, R. 1965. *Unsafe at Any Speed.* New York: Grossman.

Namier, L. B. 1929. *The Structure of Politics at the Accession of George III.* London: Macmillan.

Olson, M., Jr. 1965. *The Logic of Collective Action.* Cambridge, Mass.: Harvard University Press.

Paige, J. M. 1975. *Agrarian Revolution.* New York: Free Press.

Park, R. E., E. W. Burgess, and R. D. McKenzie. 1925. *The City.* Chicago: University of Chicago Press.

Parsons, T. 1967a. "On the Concept of Political Power." In *Sociological Theory and Modern Society*, 297–354. New York: Free Press.

———. 1967b. "Some Reflections on the Place of Force in Social Process." In *Sociological Theory and Modern Society*, 264–96. New York: Free Press.

Perrow, C. 1984. *Normal Accidents*. New York: Basic Books.

Piore, M. J., and C. F. Sabel. 1984. *The Second Industrial Divide*. New York: Basic Books.

Pólya, G. 1957. *How to Solve It*. Garden City, N.Y.: Doubleday.

Rashevsky, N. 1968. *Looking at History through Mathematics*. Cambridge, Mass.: MIT Press.

Rothman, D. 1971. *The Discovery of the Asylum*. Boston: Little, Brown.

Sahlins, M. 1985. *Islands of History*. Chicago: University of Chicago Press.

Salaff, J. W. 1981. *Working Daughters of Hong Kong*. Cambridge: Cambridge University Press.

Sassen, S. 1991. *The Global City*. Princeton, N.J.: Princeton University Press.

Schelling, T. 1978. *Micromotives and Macrobehavior*. New York: Norton.

Simmel, G. 1950. "The Triad." In *The Sociology of George Simmel*, trans. and ed. K. H. Wolff, 145–69. Glencoe, Ill.: Free Press.

Simon, H. A. 1957. *Models of Man*. New York: John Wiley.

———. 1982. *Models of Bounded Rationality*. 2 vols. Cambridge, Mass.: MIT Press.

Spilerman, S. 1977. "Careers, Labor Market Structure, and Socioeconomic Achievement." *American Journal of Sociology* 83:551–93.

Stinchcombe, A. L. 1968. *Constructing Social Theories*. New York: Harcourt, Brace and World.

Suchman, M. C., and M. L. Cahill. 1996. "The Hired Gun as Facilitator." *Law and Social Inquiry* 21:679–712.

Suttles, G. 1968. *The Social Order of the Slum*. Chicago: University of Chicago Press.

———. 1984. "The Cumulative Texture of Local Urban Culture." *American Journal of Sociology* 90:283–304.

Szreter, S. 1984. "The Origins of the Registrar General's Social Classification of Occupations." *British Journal of Sociology* 35:522–46.

Taylor, A. J. P. 1961. *The Origins of the Second World War*. London: Hamilton.

Therborn, G. 1977. "The Rule of Capital and the Rise of Democracy." *New Left Review* 103:3–42.

Thernstrom, S. 1964. *Poverty and Progress*. Cambridge, Mass.: Harvard University Press.

Thomas, W. I., and D. S. Thomas. 1928. *The Child in America*. New York: Alfred A. Knopf.

Thomas, W. I., and F. Znaniecki. 1918–20. *The Polish Peasant in Europe and America*. 5 vols. Chicago: University of Chicago Press, and Boston: Badger.

Tocqueville, A. de. [1856] 1955. *The Old Régime and the French Revolution*. Trans. S. Gilbert. Garden City, N.Y.: Doubleday.

Vickery, A. 1998. *The Gentleman's Daughter*. New Haven, Conn.: Yale University Press.

Warner, W. L., M. Meeker, and K. Eells. 1949. *Social Class in America*. Chicago: Science Research Associates.

Warner, W. L., J. O. Low, P. S. Lunt, and L. Srole. 1963. *Yankee City*. Abridged ed. New Haven, Conn.: Yale University Press.

West, C., and D. H. Zimmerman. 1987. "Doing Gender." *Gender and Society* 1:125–51.

White, H. C. 1970. *Chains of Opportunity*. Cambridge, Mass.: Harvard University Press.

Whyte, W. F. 1943. *Street Corner Society*. Chicago: University of Chicago Press.

Wolf, Eric. 1982. *Europe and the People without History*. Berkeley: University of California Press.

INDEX